Music & Your Mind

Music
& YOUR
Mind

Listening with a New Consciousness

HELEN L. BONNY
& LOUIS M. SAVARY

Station Hill Press

Published by Station Hill Press, Inc., Barrytown, New York 12507

Distributed by The Talman Company, 150 Fifth Avenue, New York, New York 10011.

Cover design by Susan Quasha.

Library of Congress Cataloging-in-Publication Data

Bonny, Helen L.
  Music and your mind: listening with a new consciousness / Helen L. Bonny and Louis M. Savary,
      p. cm.
  ISBN 0-88268-094-3
  1. Music—Psychology. 2. Music, Influence of. I. Savary, Louis M. II. Title.
ML3920.B556 1990
781'.11—dc20   89-26294

ACKNOWLEDGMENTS

Many of the works from which selections herein are taken are protected by copyright, and may not be reproduced in any form without the consent of the authors, their publishers, or their agents. Every effort has been made to trace the ownership of all selections in this book and to obtain the necessary authorization for their use. If any errors or omissions have occurred in this regard, corrections will be made in all future editions of the book.

Thomas Bailey Aldrich, poetry quoted in *Growing Up With Music* by Hilda Hunter, Fleming H. Revell Co., copyright © 1970 by Hewitt House; Roberto Assagioli, M.D., selections from *Psychosynthesis*, Hobbs, Dorman & Co., Inc., copyright © 1965 by Psychosynthesis Research Foundation; James Baldwin, selection from *Going to Meet the Man*, The Dial Press, Inc., copyright © 1965 by James Baldwin; Leonard Bernstein, selections from *The Infinite Variety of Music*, Simon & Schuster, copyright © 1966 by Leonard Bernstein Foundation, Inc.; Carlos Chavez, selection from *Musical Thought*, Harvard University Press, copyright © 1961 by the President and Fellows of Harvard College; Aaron Copland, selections from *Copland on Music*, Doubleday & Co., Inc., copyright © 1960 by Aaron Copland; Lawrence Eisman, selections from *Making Music Your Own*, Silver Burdett Company, copyright © 1968 by General Learning Corporation; Ralph Waldo Emerson, selection quoted in *Blake's Fourfold Vision* by Harold C. Goddard, Pendle Hill, copyright © 1956 by Pendle Hill; Kahlil Gibran, selection from *The Prophet*, Alfred A. Knopf, Inc., copyright © 1923 by Kahlil Gibran and copyright © 1951 by Administrators C.T.A. of Gibran Estate and Mary G. Gibran; Herbert Glass, selection from the album jacket *The Nutcracker* by Peter Ilyich Tchaikovsky, Artia Recording Corp., copyright © 1961 by Artia Recording Corp.; Stanislav Grof, selections from "LSD and the Cosmic Game: Outline of Psychedelic Cosmology and Ontology of Being," unpublished paper, Maryland Psychiatric Research Center, copyright © 1972 by Stanislav Grof; Kate Hevner, selection from "Experimental Studies of the Elements of Expression in Music," *American Journal of Psychology*,

Contents

Author's Note

Many people are necessarily involved in the inspiration for and creation of a book such as this. *Music and Your Mind* is dedicated to the many listeners who shared their new consciousness experiences on its pages.

Special mention must be made of those who helped gather data and report case studies: foremost, workshop leaders Sister M. Trinitas Bochini and Daniel P. Brown; and facilitators Ronald Harvey, Richard Cohen and Henry Coffey. Thanks to Patty Olert for taking care of many details; to Michael Emley, M.D., director of Mantra, for his cooperation; to Thomas Hardy for arranging things at Epoch House; and to Geir Viljalmsson for helping to facilitate the Icelandic experience.

A word of gratitude to friends at the Maryland Psychiatric Research Center: Dr. Albert A. Kurland, M.D., director of the Center, for his support; John Lenox, Ph.D. for help with statistical analysis; Sandford Unger, Ph.D., for suggestions and insights; and William Richards for reading and reacting to various parts of the manuscript.

We wish to say thank you in a special way to Cecil R. Chamberlin, M.D., of the Menninger Foundation for his cooperative support of the Institute for Consciousness and Music; and to John C. Lilly, M.D., who first suggested that we two work together.

To my children, Beatrice Starrett, Erich Lind Bonny, and Francis Albert Bonny, much gratitude for their support of my work during the preparation of this book.

To Evan Pritchard, much thanks for his editorial support in the updating of this book.

Helen L. Bonny
Louis M. Savary
March 1st, 1990

Preface

The first edition of *Music and Your Mind* appeared in 1973, near the end of an era—a period of introspection, motivated by disillusionment with establishment values in government, religion and the culture. With dwindling opportunities to inspect our outer environment, explorers of the mind and the psyche searched for new worlds within. One approach involved powerful psychedelic drugs, where both profound and disturbing openings of the mind revealed the heights and depths of inner exploration. Sudden entrances into the mysteries of the mind exposed people of the 60's and 70's to experiences for which many were not adequately prepared. As a result, respected and time-tested spiritual practices designed to broaden and expand human experience were avidly sought. Gurus found groups of eager young students. But courses in spiritual development or journeys to the East did not compensate for the deficit. Visions of sublime goals could be imagined but the inability to achieve those goals without years of experience and training proved frustratingly impossible.

Pandora's box had been opened—but then what? Questions were asked, such as: How does one approach one's inner core? Are revelations of one's higher self realizable, or more important, authentic? For many the task was too difficult; the energy engendered by the search was frittered away in a headlong rush into consumerism.

Fascinated with the further reaches of human consciousness, researchers and mind explorers coined the term "altered states of consciousness" to define the psyche's parameters that were being reached. Nondrug approaches, both rediscovered and invented, were designed to investigate various levels of consciousness: hypnosis, biofeedback, and relaxation and music, to mention a few. *Music and Your Mind* was the first book to demonstrate the profound relationship between mind and music and to outline exercises and suggest musical selections to accommodate an altered state of consciousness experience.

Public recognition of imagery as a powerful tool in psychotherapy, healing, creativity, holistic growth, and in promoting self-acceptance and life-change has marked the years between publication and republication of this book. As a healing modality, the imaginal side of our nature, recognized through dreams, reverie, and artistic expression had traditionally taken second place to the exacting sciences designed to cure our ills or alleviate our distress. Recently within clinical science, however, recognition that disease may be related to stress and our modern preoccupation with mechanical and fast-paced living has changed the direction of treatment. Furthermore, the media fills our minds with pregnant, partially-digested images which lie unprocessed creating a backlog of feeling, as the press of duty carries us on to new waves of experience. The cycle continues as unfulfilled experience creates inner resistance resulting in stress, and eventually, in disease. How can we break the vicious cycle? Fortunately we can turn to clinicians who have discovered that the stress cycle can be broken by periodic practices which include relaxation, mental imagery and music.

Since the publication of *Music and Your Mind* seventeen years ago, a process of evoking imagery through music-listening has come to be called Guided Imagery and Music, GIM for short. Research in GIM dyads, one-to-one, e.g., a psychotherapist with a patient, has produced promising results in greater self-esteem, as patients come to know and understand themselves better through music and imagery exercises. The unique ability of carefully-chosen music to help a person reveal positive qualities of inner goodness, harmony, and beauty provides a holistic balance to life. It can also help us explore possible problem areas as well.

To derive the greatest benefit from GIM, a planned series of music sessions under a competent guide is recommended. For those who wish to be guides and practice GIM professionally, training programs are available. The trainee experiencing multiple personal GIM sessions learns to effectively use the procedure with others. Those who have completed such training report a valued change in overall life-perspective and satisfaction. Therefore, GIM may be used as an ongoing process by anyone who is a seeker after that truth which lies within each of us.

After a decade of study exploring the phenomena of consciousness, the usage of the term "nonordinary states of consciousness" is being questioned. We have learned that the depth and variety of an altered state of consciousness may be idiosyncratic—particular to the experiencer—and, further, that altered states in varying degree and under particular circumstances are often but a variation of the usual state. Of more interest to the current researcher is the descriptive quality of each individual GIM experience and how that experience may interact in the ongoing life of the person. What we call the "product" of the experience, which characteristically comes in the form of imagery or metaphor, often holds the key to insight and change.

Taken from the practice of hypnosis, the countdown induction, as described in *Music and Your Mind* exercises, was originally designed to carry the experiencer into deeper levels of relaxation and allow mental images to surface in consciousness. Experience has taught practitioners of GIM that the "count-down" is not generally necessary or useful. At times, a count-down may prove detrimental in that it evokes different or deeper levels of consciousness than may be appropriate for a certain traveler. A well-planned relaxation and induction will usually prove sufficient as preparation for the music portion of the session. The music itself, when carefully chosen, carries the traveler where he/she needs to go.

The practice of Guided Imagery and Music with groups has changed over the years. More recently, as music therapists have incorporated GIM into their practice, a wide variety of approaches have evolved. The reader is directed to the recent work of Lisa Summer, *GIM in the Institutional Setting*, for more detailed information on group work. For example, we have found that spoken inductions between musical selections (as described in Chapter 4, "Listening in a Group") can sometimes break an important process, create discomfort, or return travelers to a lighter state of consciousness. Therefore, in group work, the entire music program is usually played without interruption.

The introduction of the dyad into GIM work has profoundly increased its effectiveness as a therapy and as a transformational tool. In a dyad session, one person, the traveler, experiences the music, and the other person serves as a guide. The guide's duties are to provide a relaxation technique and/or induction and to choose the music. While the music plays, the guide sits close to the traveler as support, and may encourage the traveler to verbalize the imagery that is occurring. Verbalization on the part of the traveler, rather than detracting from the production of imagery, actually deepens and enhances its emotional effect. Success in

GIM depends to a great degree upon the rapport created before the session between traveler and guide, and upon the skill of the guide. Caution is suggested in using this dyadic process unless the guide has had previous and thorough training in GIM.

Specialized training is available for those desiring to learn these skills and/or for those eager to use them in a private therapeutic practice. The interested reader is encouraged to write to The Bonny Foundation for further information on workshops, resources, and training programs in Guided Imagery and Music: P.O. Box 2232, Salina, Kansas, 67402; (913)827-1497.

Aside from a thoroughly revised Appendix C: "Suggested Recordings for Altered States of Consciousness Experiences," this edition of *Music and Your Mind* is essentially identical to our original edition published by Harper and Row in 1973. As authors, delighted to see our primer on Guided Imagery and Music available again, we are grateful to the many friends and colleagues who perseveringly encouraged us to find a way to get *Music and Your Mind* back in print. In this age, when almost every publisher prefers to produce only new titles, it is heartening to know people like George and Susan Quasha at Station Hill Press who are open and courageous enough to decide that an old book like ours is worth republishing.

Introduction

Human Consciousness

This is a book about the use of music in reaching and exploring non-ordinary levels of human consciousness.

Human consciousness is like a many-storied skyscraper. Its ground floor represents normal consciousness—the state of mind we ordinarily use in thinking, problem solving, feeling, sensing, remembering, communicating, and so on. In this skyscraper of the mind there are many higher and deeper levels of consciousness—realms of creativity, insight, self-realization, deep memory, the unconscious, dreams, transpersonal and religious experience. However, few people ever go beyond the mind's first floor.

Because of widespread interest in these non-ordinary levels of human consciousness, many techniques, in addition to drugs, have been developed or re-developed to help pierce through the level of everyday consciousness. Such techniques include bio-feedback, mind control, Zen, self-hypnosis and transcendental meditation.

It is one thing to be convinced that non-ordinary levels of the mind exist and to wish to explore them; it is another to know how to find your way there. Even if you are able to find an elevator that takes you to other levels of your mind, it helps to know what to do when you get there—when, as it were, you step off the elevator.

Music and Your Mind

The objective of *Music and Your Mind* is to examine the relationship between consciousness and music by studying all three phases of inner space exploration: (1) an understanding of non-ordinary levels of consciousness, (2) techniques for going beyond ordinary consciousness, and (3) suggested exercises for individual and group exploration of the frontiers of various levels of consciousness.

Experience is the best way to know how it feels to be on another level of consciousness. As you read the experiences of others in the following pages, you will begin to realize the potential variety and expanse of the human mind. A more technical analysis of other levels of consciousness, and their relation to ordinary awareness, is suggested in Appendix A. The science of human consciousness—the geography, or geometry, of inner space—is still in its primitive stages; the cognitive models made today by psychologists are perhaps as unsophisticated as pre-Columbian maps of the world.

Techniques for reaching new levels of consciousness are described in the first chapter. They involve relaxation, concentration, and listening to suggested musical selections in an altered state of consciousness. The selections are designed for ordinary individuals and groups. They do not necessarily require a guide or guru, nor do they require the use of any drug, machine, or special electronic equipment other than a phonograph or tape recorder. The techniques do require a modicum of instruction; they can be learned from the text and its suggested methods.

The musical selections used in the book for exploring altered states are taken from commercially available LP records, some of which may already be a part of your collection.

The later chapters of the book present exercises which have as their goal helping individual listeners and groups explore their inner selves, those other floors of the mind. They are designed for beginners as well as the more advanced and they present various ways of listening to music in altered states of consciousness. Their aim is to help listeners develop self-awareness, clarify personal values, release blocked-up psychic energy sources, enrich group spirit, bring about deep relaxation, and foster religious experience.

Once you enter an altered state of consciousness, you can begin to listen to music in this new way. It will involve your total awareness, the fullest participation of your multi-dimensional self. As such a listener you will normally never entirely leave ordinary consciousness: You will continue to hear doors slam, smell food cooking, feel the temperature of the room. Yet your everyday level of awareness will grow less important because the music itself will begin to engage you on other levels of consciousness: For example, you may enter avenues of insight and creativity, centers of self-realization and self-evaluation, layers of memory and dreams, realms of religious and transpersonal experience.

These revelatory experiences have occurred, at some time or other, in most people's lives. They open provinces of the mind familiar to composers, poets, inventors, and mystics; they involve cracking through the shell of ordinary perception, stretching the capacities of cognitive mechanisms, exploring regions of transcendence and mystery. *Music and Your Mind* offers a method for everyone to open these forgotten doors.

Chapter 1

How to Reach a New Consciousness

Listening patterns

People today listen to music for a variety of reasons. Many let the radio play while they work or chat or read; for them music is a pleasant distraction. Others listen to it for fun and relaxation. Some dance to it or sing along with it. Hi-fi enthusiasts focus on sound qualities in the recording. Music students are professionally analytic. Concertgoers are attracted to it for cultural and aesthetic reasons. These are just some of the ways people listen to music.

Music furnishes a delightful recreation for the hours of respite from the cares of the day, and lasts us through life.

Thomas Jefferson

In work at the Maryland Psychiatric Research Center, it was rediscovered that there was a new way to music, an approach that brings music into special focus and uses its powers to uncover and enrich one's listening patterns. This book invites you to learn to listen in this new way—with a new awareness, with heightened consciousness. Not only can this new way to music deepen your normal listening experience, but you will learn to let the music take you to places in your mind that you perhaps never knew existed. It can lead you to ineffable experiences of grandeur and beauty.

And if there come the singers and the dancers and the flute players—buy of their gifts also. For they too are gatherers of fruit and frankincense, and that which they bring, though fashioned of dreams, is raiment and food for your soul.

Kahlil Gibran
The Prophet

At any given moment in a heightened state of consciousness the mind is able to contain many ideas and experiences. Awareness seems intensified, enlarged, while consciousness itself can become multi-dimensional, many-storied. Music seems to acquire color, shape, motion—even taste and scent. When listened to in a state of heightened awareness, music is able to generate greater levels of emotional intensity, depth and comprehensiveness: Melodies, harmonies, and rythms reveal meanings; insights into self are a common occurrence; one sees more ways to look at a problem, an idea, a person. Music seems to induce a heightened empathy with others, a sense of unity among people and things, a sensitivity for the divine.

Consciousness of self actually expands our control of our lives, and with that expanded power comes the capacity to let ourselves go. This is the truth behind the seeming paradox, that the more consciousness of

one's self one has, the more spontaneous and creative one can be at the same time.

Rollo May

Adding this new dimension to music listening can
increase the realization of your human potential and
provide a new method for getting in touch with yourself. Through insights gained via this approach, you
will be led to more vital, creative, and satisfying
living.

Music is a moral law. It gives a soul to the universe,
wings to the mind, flight to the imagination, a charm
to sadness, gaiety and life to everything. It is the
essence of order, and leads to all that is good, just,
and beautiful, of which it is the invisible, but never-
theless, dazzling, passionate, and eternal form.

Plato

New dimensions of awareness

This book is not meant for a specialized audience.
It is written for all those willing to experience new
dimensions of awareness. Its methods for listening
can be understood by people of every background.
Almost everyone can experience music in this new
way and be affected by it.

Music is not illusion, but revelation rather. Its triumphant power resides in the fact that it reveals to
us beauties we find nowhere else, and that the

apprehension of them is not transitory, but a perpetual reconcilement to life.

Piotr Ilyich Tchaikovsky

Music listened to in altered states of consciousness can bring out things in you that nothing or no one has ever previously elicited. Many describe the experience as full of insight; others find a healing force; some let the music take them to unexplored provinces of the psyche; while for others it provides a heightened awareness of their ordinary world.

Although listening to music with heightened consciousness has great therapeutic value and is employed by psychologists and psychiatrists in hospitals, clinics and experimental centers, there is no reason why extraordinary listening experiences cannot happen everywhere and be enjoyed by everyone who loves music.

The secret of all this is reaching new levels of consciousness, learning how to transcend ordinary consciousness and enter a new dimension of awareness. In the past, people who wished to have such special experiences took drugs—LSD, mescaline, marijuana, sought the help of a hypnotist, retired to monastic solitude, or became disciples of some Far Eastern school of Zen or Tao. Others, more versed in mind-tripping, used sensory deprivation, sensory overload, or perception distortion techniques.

Q. Do you think it is possible that through the conscious listening to music you could reverse the order of the creative process?

L.B. And get back to the stage the composer was in

when he wrote it, through the music you're hearing?
Is that what you're trying to say? I guess it's con-
cievable. That's a very mystical idea. I think that's
more mystical than anything I've said.

                                        Leonard Bernstein

This new way to music employs no chemical or
mechanical means to achieve altered consciousness.
The altered state is self-induced, using only the individual's body and mind. No equipment is needed,
other than a phonograph or tape recorder to play
musical selections. The technique is so simple that
anyone can learn it, even children. Many people will
find that they learn much faster with a guide, but a
guide is not essential.

We are the music makers,
and we are the dreamers of dreams.
                                        Arthur W. O'Shaughnessy

---

The book deals with four kinds of listeners. The
first and most common is the *individual listener.*
Millions of people in the world have collections of
records and tapes that they enjoy listening to. For
many of these, their musical libraries are one of the
most treasured parts of their possessions. Folk music,
pop, rock, country and western, classical, opera and
electronic music are all waiting to be experienced in
altered consciousness.

Hold this sea-shell to your ear,
  And you shall hear,

Not the andante of the sea,
Not the wild wind's symphony,
But your own heart's minstrelsy.

Thomas Bailey Aldrich

The *listening group* is the next largest set of listeners. How often have you gone to visit a friend just to listen to a new LP with him? Couples sit together and listen; groups of young people gather to hear their favorite albums. Chapter 5 suggests special ways to enhance the group experience—bringing shared enjoyment and insight through music.

Music appreciation classes in school form another group of listeners. An entire class can be led to reach a heightened consciousness and enjoy music in a new way. In classrooms, the teacher assumes the responsibility of acting as guide for the students.

Those who wish to share deep *religious experience* form a further group to whom the book is directed. Listening to music in altered states of consciousness provides a new way into spiritual and transpersonal spaces of the mind. Such use of music is not limited to professional religious people, but is open to anyone who believes in some forces or Being greater than humanity.

The superior man tries to promote music as a means to the perfection of human culture. When such music prevails, and people's minds are led towards the right ideals and aspirations, we may see the appearance of a great nation.

Confucius

Self-Inducing an Altered State of Consciousness

The unique and operative element in the new way to music is the altered state of consciousness (ASC). The first objective is to show how to achieve it—how to pass from ordinary consciousness into a non-ordinary state.

At times you will want to self-induce an altered state; at other times, you may act as guide to help others get there. These two situations are considered separately.

Though the process of self-induction may take as long as half an hour at first, after some practice people can usually self-induce an altered state in minutes. Don't be disappointed if you do not succeed during the first few tries. Maintain a positive attitude and view every element of partial success as a reason for optimism. As ASC becomes a familiar part of your mental repertoire, you will find your body and mind looking forward to the experience.

We allow our eyes and ears, mouth, nose, hands, feet —our whole sensitized surface, antenna-like—just to be the entrance doors through which impressions, sensations, odors, tastes and sounds enter us, there to be received, absorbed and digested by our whole self. We practice sitting quietly, with eyes closed and becoming receptive to whatever sounds may reach us (slight stirrings, voices, wind or rain, music next door, street noises, etc.) without trying to identify and label them immediately, **but letting them freely enter us and be experienced.**

Charlotte Selver

Entrance into altered states requires (1) relaxation and (2) concentration. These two skills must be mastered in order to enjoy the new way to music. At first, learning to relax and concentrate requires constant practice. Once learned, however, these skills become natural and their performance easy.

① Relaxation

Many people think that relaxation means lying limp, with arms and legs flaccid and heavy. Quite the contrary: To feel relaxed is to feel weightless.

Feeling weightless means that the body's muscles are in equilibrium or balance. Muscles come in pairs —one designed to push out, the other to pull back. When these muscle pairs are in balance—neither pulling nor pushing, yet ready to go either way— they are in equilibrium, and that particular part of the body feels weightless. When the muscles of the entire body are in this state of balance or weightlessness, the body is totally relaxed.

Most techniques use a variety of methods for relaxing. Zen meditation, behavior modification, transcendental meditation, mind control, Gestalt therapy, hypnosis, and other disciplines—all have their approaches. If you are familiar with any of these relaxation techniques and you find that they help you, by all means use them.

Many of these disciplines are designed to help the student achieve a passage from ordinary to nonordinary consciousness. The mental pathway to a meditation space is much the same as that to a music listening space.

Comfort is the first objective. The most successful positions for relaxing seem to be sitting or lying down, although other relaxation disciplines use the body in different ways. Yoga, for example, utilizes a wide variety of postures to generate bodily and mental poise.

Most people find they relax best by lying supine on a floor, sofa, or bed. It is simple enough to lie down flat on one's back, but systematic relaxation requires the aid of the mind. To relax, an individual must consciously suggest that his body relax. Most teachers advise a simple procedure: Begin by fixing the mind on the feet and relax them; then the legs, the arms, abdomen, chest, throat, facial muscles, and eyes. Each in turn should yield to suggestion until complete relaxation is achieved. Some people prefer to begin the relaxation process at the head, and from there work down to their toes.

You may find it helpful to accompany this process with a key word or phrase. For example, when fixing the mind on the feet, say "Relax now" in a quiet voice. Repeat the suggestion until the feet feel relaxed. Then transfer your attention to the legs, and follow the same procedure. Using a favorite phrase is a way of helping the mind fixate. The words also act as a trigger the next time you wish to relax. Your body will remember the feeling it discovered when you first used the phrase, and will generate a similar feeling the next time, with much less effort.

An important part of relaxation is breath flow. There is no need to increase or lengthen respiration or to do special breathing exercises. Simply try to maintain an even rhythm in your breathing. Regular rhythmic inhalation and exhalation will help a great deal in securing complete relaxation, not only of the body but of the mind as well. Before every listening experience, relax your body as completely as possible. Develop a pattern for bringing on this quietly balanced state, and practice it often. The more complete the relaxation, the deeper will be the listening experience.

Concentration

Once the body is relaxed, the mind is ready to concentrate. Of course, concentration was also required to effect relaxation of the body: You have already been concentrating.

Concentration means attention. Think of your mind as the lens of a camera focused on an object—say, a rose. Let your mind, like the camera, fix itself on the rose. Let there be nothing else in the world but the rose—nothing else to see but its color and shape, nothing else to smell but its fragrance, nothing else to hear but its silence.

Don't try to analyze, describe, or define the flower. Simply identify it—acknowledge its uniqueness. Keep your mind on the rose until you could recognize it anywhere. Practice concentrating until, even with your eyes closed, you can "see" every detail of the rose.

In all this, there should be no forcing or straining. Your mind can concentrate best when you are relaxed. Relaxation and concentration always go together.

Practice concentration at odd moments during the day—while waiting for someone or while riding a bus. In the beginning, choose a concrete object to focus upon—a flower, a burning candle, or a piece of fruit. Later, your mind will be able to create its own objects. Every time you exercise your mind power you are preparing yourself for fuller listening experience.

Many teachers recommend the sounding of a word
or syllable—yogis often suggest the syllable "om"—
to help bring a restless mind to attention. Humming
or intoning a single note, and holding it, sets up a
vibration which affects the entire body, and helps it
to respond to a constant frequency.

**From the repeating word effect, I learned something
about going with the flow, relaxing and allowing
instructions from some place else to run my bio-
computer. If one relaxes totally while listening to the
repeating word, one can quickly find all of the phenomena that I have described above. However, if one
is "up tight" and refuses to really "let go" even
though one would like to let go, these phenomena
just do not occur as frequently.**

John C. Lilly

As you advance in the art of concentration, enlarge
the repertoire of your objects of concentration. Place
an acorn before you and gaze steadily at it, fixing
its attributes firmly in your mind. Then imagine the
acorn beneath the ground, see its burst seed and a
root shooting out from it. Next see the first green
leaf; finally, the complete tree. Don't hurry the process: Let nothing interfere until in your mind the
acorn has become a towering oak.

**But that which occupies the most prominent place in
Bach's work is pictorial poetry. Above everything
else he seeks the picture, and in this respect he is
very different from Wagner, who is rather a lyric**

dramatist. Bach himself is nearer to Berlioz, and nearer still to Michelangelo. If it had been possible for him to see a picture by Michelangelo, doubtless he would have found in him something of his own soul.

But his contemporaries remained unaware of his painter's soul. His pupils and his sons did not perceive his pictorial instincts, any more than they suspected that his true greatness was as a musical poet.

Albert Schweitzer

Traditionally, these relaxation and concentration techniques are used to lead to meditation and prayer. The purpose here is to listen to music with a new consciousness, although the listener may in fact be led to new depths of religious experience.

The Induction

With the body relaxed and the mind concentrating, you are to ready to begin the induction. An altered state of consciousness is like a new level of awareness: To reach it requires a displacement of the center of consciousness from its normal area of activity on the main floor to a different floor. Such displacement involves movement; hence, most people visualize it as "going up" or "going down." Some like to imagine a staircase, an escalator, or an elevator to facilitate the induction.

For example, suppose that the goal of your induction is a summer meadow where you will listen to some restful music. Begin by visualizing yourself standing at a doorway. You open the door and, before you in the soft twilight mist, you see a winding stone staircase. As you move from one step to the next, count slowly from ten down to zero. At each count, suggest to yourself that the mist will soon disappear and you will sense the warm sunlight of your meadow approaching. When you reach zero, allow yourself to feel the change: Your feet are now walking on soft grass; you feel the gentle touch of a cool breeze; you hear the rustling leaves and the chirping of birds. You are now entering a new level of consciousness and are ready to let the music take you wherever it wants you to go.

March of the Great Staircase: It is a big staircase, a very big one. It has more than one thousand steps, all in ivory. It is very beautiful. Nobody dares use it, for fear of spoiling it. Even the King has never used it. To leave his room, he jumps out of the window. And very often he says: I love this stairway so dearly that I shall have it stuffed. Wouldn't you feel that way too?

Erik Satie

Similar inductions will be presented before some of the exercises in the following chapters. You will soon learn which type is most effective for you.

At times, you may not be satisfied with the level of consciousness achieved—because of distractions, or because of insufficient relaxation and concentration. You may want to enter a deeper state before listening to further music selections. In such cases, the induction may be repeated or continued by reinforcing the induction images (a new stairway) and repeating the countdown.

On rare occasions, you may find it simply impossible to induce even the lightest experience of a changed consciousness. When this happens, don't force or strain in any way. Simply play the music as if you *were* in an ASC. Meanwhile, suggest to yourself that you will look forward to the experience next time. Such an accepting attitude is often enough to bring about a spontaneous alteration of consciousness.

In an Altered State of Consciousness

In early practice sessions, people may be surprised—or disappointed—to discover that they are not overwhelmed with new feelings or transported into states of ectasy. In fact, they sometimes report that they don't *feel* any different. A light trance state is usually characterized by a sense of being hyper-aware of the music.

Lucy: If you use your imagination, you can see lots of things in the cloud formations . . . What do you think you see, Linus?
Linus: Well, those clouds up there look to me like the map of the British Honduras on the Caribbean.
That cloud up there looks a little like the profile of Thomas Eakins, the famous painter and sculptor . . .
And that group of clouds over there gives me the impression of the stoning of Stephen . . . I can see the Apostle Paul standing there to one side . . .
Lucy: Uh, huh . . . That's very good . . . What do you see in the clouds, Charlie Brown?
Charlie Brown: Well, I was going to say I saw a ducky and a horsie, but I changed my mind!
Charles Schultz

Some people fear a loss of self-control in an altered state of consciousness, but rarely will anyone in ASC do anything he would not be willing to do in ordinary consciousness. Furthermore, unless you specifically block out external distractions, you will remain aware of everything happening around you. The ringing of a telephone, the cry of a child, the smell of something burning would be recognized and responded to.

A person in an altered state seldom loses consciousness of self. He knows what is happening around him at all times. He may walk or even dance while still remaining in an altered state, though usually a less intense one. In very deep states, however, the limbs may tend to go limp. It is usually inadvisable to engage in activities requiring physical dexterity during such deep states—driving a car, for example.

The unconscious differs from the conscious mind in that it tends to accept as fact any idea presented to it. Because of this, suggestions of feeling or events made while in heightened consciousness tend to assume greater reality. Thus, a listener may be able to perceive music as color, shape and movement; melodic sequences can evoke scenes from real life or fantasy; rhythmic patterns can elicit emotions of love, joy, union, loneliness, fear, grief; inspirational music can encourage deep religious experience. The altered state of consciousness can do all this with music in a way that ordinary consciousness never could.

**Summer ends now; now barbarous in beauty,
   the stock rise
Around; up above, what wind-walks!**

what lovely behaviour
Of silk-sack clouds! Has wilder, willful-waiver
Meal-drift moulded ever and melted across skies?
                              Gerard Manley Hopkins
                              Hurrahing in Harvest

Memories are an important source of material for the workings of the altered consciousness. The unconscious mind can remember in complete detail everything in an individual's personal history, including events which the conscious mind has totally forgotten. With the help of appropriate music, sets of memories can be resurrected and recombined to produce completely new experiences.

Although there are certain similarities between listening to music under hallucinogenic drugs and in a self-induced altered state of consciousness, the two states differ in several respects. A person under the influence of an hallucinogen normally remains in an altered state of consciousness for many hours; a self-induced changed state will last only as long as the subject chooses. He is so completely in control of the situation that he can terminate it at any moment. Children in school seem to be satisfied with an experience lasting five to seven minutes. Adults are capable of remaining in an altered state for hours on end (for example, during an entire opera).

Sometimes the altered state *must* be interrupted for one reason or another. In such cases, you may hold it in abeyance during the interruption, by suggesting to yourself that when you return to the music you will simply count from one to three and find yourself back where you had been before the break. In fact, you may well give this suggestion to yourself before you begin listening when you anticipate an interruption.

The exercises in this book are perfectly safe for anyone to perform if they are carried out according to instructions, and with healthy, positive motivation. People who are emotionally disturbed, deeply depressed, or under psychiatric care should not use self-induced ASC without professional assistance or approval.

Return to Normal Consciousness

Research experts in altered states of consciousness recommend that return to normal consciousness follow a pattern. Consequently, each of the exercises in *Music and Your Mind* concludes with a short procedure to bring the listener back to ordinary consciousness. This has three advantages: First, it provides a simple pattern for returning to ordinary consciousness which can be used in all situations; second, it insures that on returning to normal consciousness you will feel alert, rested, and charged with positive emotions; third, it reinforces the path between normal and altered consciousness, so that subsequent returns to the new consciousness become easier to effect.

A termination procedure might run as follows: "The music has ended and I am ready to return to normal consciousness. I will now count from three to zero; when I reach zero I will open my eyes and be in my normal consciousness, fully rested and alert, and deeply satisfied by the experience." You may want to recapitulate the insights gained during the session, and tell yourself that you will be able to recall them easily whenever you wish. You may also suggest that you will remember the pathway or procedure by which you entered this particular listening space in your mind, and be able to find it quickly whenever you wish to return.

Although it is almost always easier to return to an altered state once you have been there, it is still a good idea to include the suggestion to remember the pathway that led to the new space in your mind. Experts recommend that both the induction and termination procedures—no matter how short—be a part of every experience in an altered state.

Don't be discouraged if your efforts fail in the beginning. Continue to practice; your technique will improve each time. Many people require several attempts before noting any signs of success. Remember that most of us are unfamiliar with the workings of our unconscious mind. However, with repetition and ritual, the inner mind will eventually open its gates and invite you in. Once inside, you will discover a vast terrain with many areas to explore. The mind is still largely uncharted territory; we are all pilgrims there.

Man appears to be the most complex and complicated phenomenon in the over-all scheme of the cosmic game.

Stanislav Grof

The inner mind has its own laws. Time may be transformed with altered consciousness: It may pass so quickly that several hours of clock time seem like as many minutes. On other occasions, a single musical note may seem endless! The rules of logic do not apply in the new states of consciousness. Your inner mind, like the Red Queen in *Alice in Wonderland*, may readily "believe at least six impossible things before breakfast."

Within the province of the mind, what I believe to be true is true or becomes true, within the limits to be found experientially and experimentally. These limits are further beliefs to be transcended. This is the major thing to be said about all inner trips, by LSD, by meditation, by hypnosis, by Gestalt therapy, by encounter group work, by dreaming, by isolation-solitude-confinement.

John Lilly

Remember especially that the unconscious likes *repetition.* Tell your inner self over and over that you would like to go wherever the music leads. Always be *polite,* even when you address your own unconscious. Always be *positive,* focusing your suggestions on the things you want to experience, not those you want to avoid. Always be *precise,* for the unconscious prefers simple, clear requests to vague ambiguous ones.

Group Induction

To induce altered states of consciousness in a group of people requires fundamentally the same procedure as that used for self-induction, except that one member of the group acts as guide or "facilitator" for the rest.

It is important, therefore, that the guide provide an induction sufficiently general to help each member of the group reach heightened consciousness. There are many group induction procedures, and you will find several examples later in this book. After an initial trial-and-error period, groups, like individuals, gravitate toward the procedure that proves most successful.

Even in a group, it is best for each participant to learn to self-induce the new state, leaving the guide with only the task of setting the scene for the listening experience. The guide must be aware of the individual needs of his group's members. An individual listener who self-induces altered consciousness may move at his own pace, giving himself the necessary reinforcement and encouragement as needed. Since members of a group will not all reach the same depth at the same speed, the guide must be prepared to cope with the resulting timing problems.

If the group is small enough, the guide can ask each member to raise a hand or give some agreed sign on reaching the altered state of consciousness. But with large groups it may be impractical to wait for the slow members. Also, groups often include one or two individuals who consciously refuse to enter an altered state.

With practice, the guide will learn to recognize the outward signs indicating altered consciousness in the group members. Until he has acquired this expertise, it is a good idea, during the discussion following the musical experience, to ask individuals how they had fared, what they had missed, or what had worked best. These comments will help him to improve his induction technique.

The group leader's induction responsibilities are
four-fold:

(1) To clarify the *goal* or purpose of the exercise
—whether it be precise (for example, to work
through a grief experience) or vague and general (to have a quiet listening experience);

(2) To see that each member is settled comfortably
and helped to relax completely;

✕ (3) To suggest an appropriate object or scene for
concentration to those group members who
have difficulty in focusing their mind; and

(4) To lead the group members, usually by *countdown*, into their listening spaces or altered
states of consciousness.

Although the settings and images may vary with
each occasion, these four steps form the basic structure of every group induction.

The effects of induction vary according to the dis-
positions of individual group members. One participant may be highly suggestible and enter into a
deep space almost immediately; another may be pre-
occupied with worry and hardly hear the induction;
a third may find the guide's voice annoying and be
unable to relax; a fourth may be able to reach only
a slightly altered state. Some may defiantly refuse
to enter a different level of consciousness: Those
familiar with drug-induced "highs" may be expecting
a similar experience; still others may know so little
about other levels of consciousness that they cannot
recognize a change in themselves.

The best way to deal with group induction problems is to anticipate them whenever possible. For example, the concluding part of a talk given to a re-
gional meeting of music therapists in New Jersey,

was an attempt at group induction with members of the audience. The purpose was to get them to experience at first hand what had been talked about. To avoid a poor experience for those who were genuinely interested, those who did not want to participate in the experiment were invited to stay and observe, but out of consideration for the others, to be very quiet—no talking or moving about. It was emphasized that it would be more fun to go along with the others, however. Then the procedure to be followed was explained in detail to help each listener decide whether to be a participant or an observer.

It is helpful always to offer potential participants some acceptable alternative, so that the listening experience can proceed without conflict or constraint. The very fact of having a choice may encourage the hesitant to participate.

When the group members have reached non-ordinary levels of consciousness, the guide describes a setting in which they can begin listening to the music. A number of such settings are provided in the exercises in the following chapters. The purpose of the setting is to engage the imagination, feelings, and senses in a manner that resonates with the music.

The setting or experience suggested for the group must always be presented in a positive, hopeful way. Music has the power to strengthen and intensify whatever emotion or mood the listener is exploring. Hence, positive, healthful moods are to be encouraged. Subjects will bring enough negative feelings with them to the experience and do not need any reinforcement of these. For example, although a positive treatment could be developed on the subject of loneliness, it is better to avoid focusing on it as a theme; rather, present the setting as a *search for personal meaning,* and let loneliness emerge in true perspective as a subordinate theme.

The potential richness of the listening experience should always be emphasized—the insights to be gained, the moods to be explored, the events to be savored.

Emotions such as grief and sorrow can be positive and healthy when presented in a constructive way.

The value of a work of art, what we call its beauty, lies, generally speaking, in its power to bestow happiness.

Wilhelm Worringer

Treat the setting as a point of departure, not as a rigid framework for the entire exercise. Flexibility is especially important in a group exercise, since individual participants will react to the setting with different degrees of intensity and enthusiasm. As each one allows the music to lead wherever it wishes, the original setting may become modified or even transformed into something entirely different.

While the music plays, the guide has no active duties. It is wise, however, for him to keep a watch on the listeners' responses. There may be bodily movements, changes of breathing patterns, murmurs, sighs, or smiles, although most people remain relatively motionless and silent.

Group Termination

Since group members may be presumed to be at different levels of consciousness when the music ends, the termination procedure should be sufficiently comprehensive to cover the needs of most participants.

First of all, tell the participants clearly that the music is finished; it helps to ready them for re-emergence. Next, ask them to prepare themselves for the return to normal consciousness. Tell them that you will help them to do this in a satisfying way, so that they will lose none of the positive experiences they had while listening to the music.

Then, begin the count-out. Count slowly from ten to one to make sure that even those in deep states of consciousness will have enough time to return completely to normal space.

As you count from ten to one, suggest, between numbers, that they will return alert and rested, that they will be able to recall all their insights and experiences, that they will be able clearly to formulate the ideas they wish to share with the other members of the group, that they will remember the pathway to their listening space and be able to return there easily on future occasions.

After a particularly intense experience, some people may not have returned completely to ordinary consciousness even after a long count-out. The guide will recognize this by an attitude of remoteness or lack of participation in group discussion. In such cases, the guide should address specific questions directly to these individuals. The questions require reactivation of the everyday mental machinery, which usually will rapidly restore normal consciousness.

The Group Discussion

Sharing experiences when the music has finished is one of the most satisfying and revealing elements of a group listening session. Participants usually need the guide to initiate the discussion. He should share with them his feelings concerning the experience, and elicit from them descriptions of their own experiences.

Most people will have had emotional insights during the listening session. Every effort should be made to help them feel free to express their responses if they wish. Of course, no one should be forced to participate against his will. Sometimes the listeners' experiences are quite personal or so extraordinary that they feel reluctant to talk about them. The guide, and the group members, should respect this reluctance.

For a particularly reluctant group, the guide should start the discussion with a few nonthreatening questions, such as: "How did the music affect you when it first began;" "Did your setting change in any way while it was playing;" "Were you happy when it ended;" "Did the altered state of consciousness feel any different from your ordinary state of consciousness?"

The guide may use further questions, such as:

(1) Was this a new kind of music listening experience for you? If not, describe previous similar experiences.

(2) Did you have visual imagery? Was it people, events, or nature scenes? Describe them.

(3) Did the music produce feeling states in you that were different from those induced by your usual form of listening? If so, how different

were those feelings, and how strong?

(4) Were you less aware of your surroundings than usual—of other people, extraneous noises, your own body? Did you feel that you were in a different world? What was it like?

(5) Did you see colors while listening? If so, were they in geometric designs, or were they associated with nature? Did they change with the musical phrases?

(6) Did you think at all about instrumental combinations, or the solo parts? If you did recognize these, did they take on a certain significance or form, a certain meaning?

(7) Was the experience pleasant? Unpleasant? Do you know why it was one or the other?

(8) Would you like to try this type of listening experience again? Would you change the procedure in any way?

Summary

A summary of the stages in an altered states experience is given in the following table.

Inducing Altered States of Consciousness for Individuals and Groups

Stages	Self-Induction (Carried out by individual listener)	Group-Induction (Suggested to individual listeners by guide)
Induction	Relaxation Concentration Count-down	Relaxation Concentration Count-down
Exercise	Setting Listening	Setting Listening
Termination	Count-out (3 to 1)	Count-out (10 to 1)
Reflection	Personal Reflection	Group Sharing

Chapter 2

The Individual Listener

Heightened-Awareness Listening

Depending on situation and mood, music can evoke different feelings at different times. Some might even say that the same music is actually *heard* differently at different times.

After the first piano pieces, which had kept me in a state of rapture, the artist rose, bowed as the entire assembly applauded, disappeared behind a door, came back when the applause did not die down, disappeared again, came back, disappeared. Finally there was silence. People studied the rest of the program. The women offered each other bonbons. I could not understand why all these people, after having applauded so heartily, did not remain like me, under the spell of what they had heard, and how they could resume their chatter . . .
Never could I have imagined such flexibility. The display of virtuosity at the end took my breath away. It was for me a sudden revelation of the possibilities of the piano. On the way home I walked as in a dream.

Albert Schweitzer

One of the most important rules to follow in listening to music in altered consciousness is the *iso principle*. "Iso" means "the same as" or "matching." The iso principle states that, at the beginning of a listening experience, best results are obtained when the mood of the music matches the mood of the listener. If you are feeling carefree and gay, don't listen to *March Slav* or "Mars," (The Bringer of War) from Holst's *Planets.* On the other hand, if you have been in an angry mood all day, and those feelings are still bottled up inside you, don't begin by playing Tony Scott's *Music for Zen Meditation,* which requires a state of deep tranquility.

The presence or absence of meaning, and the particular quality of the meaning in any music is dependent on a number of factors: the form and structure of the music itself, the attitude of the listeners, their previous experience, their training, talent and temperament, and their momentary mood and physiological condition . . .
The suggestiveness of music does not depend directly on the amount of formal training which the listener has had, but is apparent both to the trained and untrained.

Kate Hevner

It is as if the mind and feelings were vibrating at a certain frequency and are most satisfied with music that is attuned to that frequency.

Playing music that matches one's feelings is a help in reaching altered states of consciousness, even if the mood is not a strongly positive one. Once deeply into the altered state, the mood of the music may gradually be changed. Music may be used either to sustain a mood or to alter it.

No one can hear the Fifth Symphony, the "Halleluia Chorus," or the preludes to Lohengrin and Parsifal and remain quite the same personality as before. I do not refer to any specific healing qualities of music or art—I simply mean that self-destruction is combatted by anything which draws from us some further flow of the love that is implicit in joy.

Karl Menninger

Unpredictability

Most people who show interest in listening in altered states of consciousness at first express fears of what might happen to them in this new state. "I'd be happy to try," said one prospective listener, "if I knew I had enough control over the situation, over my mind and feelings." Another said, "I'd do it, if I were sure I wouldn't have a bad experience."

There are spaces in our minds that we are unwilling to explore. We resist entering these areas because we suspect they will reveal frightening, fearful, shameful, disgusting, or discouraging things about us.

I am told to my surprise that there are people who have never seen a goblin. One cannot help feeling sorry for such people. I am sure there must be something wrong with their eyes.

Axel Munthe

Listeners often discover mind spaces they never knew existed. Some of these contain negative elements, but the unconscious tends readily to transform the negative images into positive ones.

Whatever happens it is all right if only one is healthy; for happiness consists—entirely in the imagination.

Wolfgang Amadeus Mozart

The experience of Shirley, a young mother with three children, is not untypical. While listening to Scriabin's *Poem of Ecstasy* in an altered state of consciousness, she became a tiger. Later, in response to this threatening experience, her own fantasy created a solution. For her, the listening experience became an exercise in unpredictability.

Throughout the music I was alternately a tiger or my usual self. I was leaping from ridge to ridge among black snow-covered mountains. Then came the pause when, still a tiger, I saw my two cubs playing in the grass on a plateau by a stream. I got them food and then they alternately played and followed me. Then I became myself again and I saw the gold crown at the top of the mountain. I thought there needed to be some reason for going to the top of the mountain. My cubs wouldn't follow, so I went alone. On the way up I saw my kitten. He didn't want to go with me either and ended up falling off the cliff. But as I watched him fall, feeling helpless, suddenly a parachute opened and he reached the bottom safely. I continued to the top and got my crown, and leaped around the mountain tops again, alternately a person and a tiger. Then I returned to the waiting cubs, and somehow we all proceeded together, stopping to catch fish, swimming in the mountain streams, gamboling in the grass. I had a deep contented feeling when the music was over. It was odd, the way I changed from a tiger to myself all through the music. The imagery was very vivid, with beautiful colors and settings.

The man who looks at a canvas or listens to music is passive, but he is passive only to the extent that he is unable to create. For in listening to the music he is active; he is going through the same needs of expression, and the same self-projection, that the creator went through. It has been repeatedly said that the listener likes the music in which he finds himself, in which he recognizes his own emotions and tastes.

Carlos Chavez

Another listener described an experience which involved some surprises for her:

A lot of things happened to me. When I came out of a town and saw in the distance some land with mountains, I could tell that it was a city. I wanted to go there because none of my experiences before had included any people. I felt that it was about time to include some. There was an ocean and I had to swim across it. I knew that I wasn't a good swimmer and I thought, "This will take forever." I made myself think that it wasn't too far and that it wasn't really water, so I just walked across it. I got to the city but there were no people. I started walking around trying to find some people, but it got very misty. I thought to myself, "How am I going to find my way out of here?" I was standing with this mist around me and it began moving like a whirlpool. Suddenly I realized that the mist was a person. I later saw that it was a woman, an older woman. I looked again and saw she was my sister, my twin. It's one thing when you're looking for someone, but it's another when you find something that you weren't even looking for. I wasn't expecting her.

Unconscious listening is more dependable. Carlyle maintained that if you "see deep enough . . . you see musically; the heart of nature being everywhere musical, if you can only reach it." In signifying only itself, music becomes a language translatable by the universal awareness latent in everything. This most complex of expressions is also the oldest and so appeals to our most primitive level, inexplicable through reason. At that level we all hear music the same way.

Ned Rorem

A Variety of Experiences

Music evokes different kinds of reactions in different people at different times. While listening in altered consciousness, some people experience simply a *visual setting*. They note details in the surroundings and respond to them; usually a dominant mood or feeling pervades the experience. In this category of experiences, there is no story line or plot.

For example, one listener reported that while listening to Debussy's "Girl With the Flaxen Hair" she felt peaceful and happy. She described the images accompanying her mood.

The pond seemed to be in a clearing; the water was very calm, and still. Around the clearing was a thick forest. I could see myself in this scene. I was with someone else, someone I did not recognize. We were in a rowboat gliding across the pond. Swallows were flying and dipping above the pond. I didn't communicate with the person. The strongest colors were green and brown, the sky was blue. It was like twilight.

Some listeners experience merely colors, sensations and moods without corresponding visual fantasies. Such experiences are usually no less significant or memorable than any others, and are sometimes indicators of activity at deeper levels of consciousness. One man who listened to music for almost half an hour reported seeing nothing but a deep blue cloudless sky, and being overwhelmed by feelings of peace and tranquility. The experience had a great impact on him and he has mentioned it more than once, wishing he were able to return there.

The "Pastoral" Symphony of Beethoven, if it were called the "Kafka Metamorphosis" Symphony of Beethoven, but had all the same notes, could quite possibly be interpretable as a "Kafka" Symphony and not a "Pastoral" Symphony at all. The very fact that Beethoven says, "I'm writing a Pastoral Symphony that was inspired by happy feelings in the country," doesn't mean that it is pastoral music. What's pas-

toral about it? It's pastoral only because you've been told it's pastoral.

Leonard Bernstein

Another listener reported an experience with music in altered consciousness in which she spent the entire time floating in a river of color. From time to time she would begin to sink downward, but a few moments later she would rise again. She experienced the floating as relaxing and refreshing; the sinking, however, made her feel a bit frightened. She felt reassured again as soon as she began to rise.

While listening in altered states of consciousness, some people experience a series of images that seem unrelated on the level of ordinary consciousness. One college student, an art major, reported:

> *I found myself involved with a variety of images, not particularly continuous, such as a whirlpool, Viking ships, dancing women. (My body felt as though it were strenuously dancing with each musical inflection.) But there was no story line, nor were there any recognizable people.*

In a discussion afterwards, she was able to recognize that the succession of images she experienced were, in fact, related on a *symbolic level* and manifested a desire to express strong and graceful physical movement. The listening experience allowed her to satisfy this desire ("My body felt as though it were strenuously dancing") and she returned to ordinary consciousness feeling relaxed and rested.

Another kind of experience with symbolic imagery is the *symbolic story*. Because such symbolic events could never happen in ordinary consciousness, they are sometimes confusing or frustrating. For example, another college student reported:

> When I searched for the source, it was a small pool at the top of a large mountain. Try as I might, I could not reach the mountaintop. However, I soon found myself up there, and I don't know how I got there. The pool was as deep as the mountain was high. I dived into it and swam to the very bottom, and walked out of a door at the bottom of the mountain. Strange!

In a discussion afterward, she was able to understand the symbolism of the experience. The pool at the mountaintop clearly represented the "source" of strength or meaning in her life. She was unable to reach it by her own efforts, but paradoxically found herself there without knowing how she arrived. As soon as she begins to explore the source, by diving into the pool, she finds herself back at the foot of the mountain, where she began in a state of helplessness, unable to reach her source. The source, which is effortlessly attainable to her inner self, is elusive to her ordinary consciousness.

All I know about music is that not many people ever really hear it. And even then, on the rare occasions when something opens within, the music enters, what we mainly hear or hear corroborated, are personal, private, vanishing evocations.

James Baldwin
Sonny's Blues

Upon reflection, such listening experiences provide insights into the self which can be grasped immediately. Other more extended symbolic stories require greater reflection and discussion to extract the symbolic meaning. For adequate interpretation, it may sometimes be necessary to be aware of important events in the listener's personal history or his relationships with people significant in his life, as in the following example.

Linda's listening experience exposed her conflicting feelings toward parents, home, the expectations of others. Throughout her experience, she reported feelings of confusion, of attraction and repulsion.

I was in a meadow of waist-deep green grass. I was in a long white dress running toward a white house that seemed to be home for me. But even though I kept running, I didn't want to reach the house. I was somewhat angry and confused by the house episode. If it hadn't been for the music, I think I would have really been frightened. The music kept me going. I was alone. I saw myself running. I didn't recognize the house, but was sure it was home. I wanted to get out of the conflict that I was involved in. I would have wanted to stay in the meadow if the house hadn't been there . . .

The meadow's waist-high grass is a symbol of nature and freedom. To Linda the house represents restrictions, expected behavior, and—especially—parental or authority figures. The conflict is so strong and clear that she brings it to speech. The music takes her to another scene.

Then I found myself at a crossroads of two streams. On the four corners stood women in white dresses, who were dancing. I was made to feel somewhat unhappy by the presence of these ladies, but there wasn't much I could do about it! . . .

The imagery in this scene, again, provoked unhappy feelings. The women on the four banks had her "cornered." The authority figures in whose presence she felt uncomfortable at this "crossroads" in her life may be symbols of the many religious sisters who are her professors at college. While from one perspective she felt uncomfortable in their presence, she also identified with them in some way, for they were wearing white dresses like her.

Her next fantasy experience involved a young man she had just met that very day. He was someone with whom she could relate in a non-authoritative way.

At this point there was a fantasy involving Greg. He was in tails and I was in a long, white formal. We wanted to go out to dinner. We called people and asked them if we could come. Finally we were on a street knocking on a door. We were invited in, so we went in and ate. Neither of us knew the people. I was angered at the fact that we had to dress formally for dinner. The only other things I remember while eating were finger bowls.

As the experience continued, the message coming from the inner self became clear: Anger at the demands of formality pervading her life was coming out. Expected behavior seemed to inhibit her knowing other people.

The scene changed finally to a conversation between herself and her father where she spoke her feelings honestly.

The next scene involved my father. We were in a kitchen and he was sitting on a deacon's bench and I was standing. I was trying to explain to him how I didn't mind if I ever hurt someone physically, but I'd be hurt if I knew someone was hurt because of what I did. I was frustrated because my father wouldn't understand.

Father, sitting on a deacon's bench, is the symbol of an authority that refuses to understand her. Her conflict is clear: How can I accept and trust directives for living from a source that refuses to understand me? The conflict, now clarified symbolically, is clearly within her.

Beethoven's finest works are the enactment of a triumph—a triumph of affirmation in the face of the human condition. Beethoven is one of the great yea-sayers among creative artists; it is exhilarating to share his clear-eyed contemplation of the tragic sum of life. His music summons forth our better nature; in purely musical terms Beethoven seems to be exhorting us to Be Noble, Be Strong, Be Great in Heart, yes, and Be Compassionate. These ethical precepts we subsume from the music, but it is the music itself —the nine symphonies, the sixteen string quartets, the thirty-two piano sonatas—that holds us, and holds us in much the same way each time we return to it.

Aaron Copland

Chapter 3

Exercises for the Individual

Getting Ready

To insure a successful listening experience in an altered state, it is important that you be relaxed in the sense that the muscles are in equilibrium, neither tense nor flaccid. With practice, you will find the techniques best suited to bring about this readiness of the muscles. As you become accustomed to entering different levels of consciousness, your body will require less and less immediate preparation for listening in this way. The pathways from normal to altered states of consciousness will become increasingly familiar and open.

The following listening exercises presume you have found a satisfying and effective way to relax and induce new levels of consciousness.

Exercises that center around the meadow image are inspired by the "standard situations" developed by Hanscarl Leuner, M.D., and described in his article, "Guided Affective Imagery (GAI).*

*American Journal of Psychotherapy (January, 1969)

Exercise: The Meadow

Musical suggestions:

Beethoven, Symphony #6, 2nd movement, "By the Brook"
Delius, "Song of the Cuckoo"
Ravel, Daphnis and Chloe, #2
Cat Stevens, "Morning is Broken"

As the music begins, transport yourself to a beautiful meadow. It is your favorite time of year. Let the music, like a gentle breeze, take you all around the meadow and help you notice important details— the color of the flowers, the moisture of the earth, the rough texture of the bark of a tree, the pattern of its branches.

Let the music evoke your feelings as you enjoy this scene. Perhaps it will bring back images and feelings that are important and satisfying to you. Dwell on these images which the music shows you and discover the meaning which they have for you. Don't force or strain in any way. Let the music suggest what to do and what to think or feel. When you feel that your experience is complete, simply count three-to-one, open your eyes, and you are back in your ordinary everyday surroundings.

Exercise: The Mountain

Musical suggestions:

Brahms, Symphony #1, 2nd movement
Debussy, Nocturnes, "Sirenes"
Grofe, Grand Canyon Suite, "Sunrise"
Mahler, Symphony #4, "Ruhvell"
Rodgers & Hammerstein, The Sound of Music, "Climb Every Mountain," "Edelweiss"

As the music begins, you are in a peaceful meadow. You find a narrow path leading gently upward. Follow this path. Walk along it. Let it take you further and further, higher and higher. Without any strain or fatigue on your part, the music carries you along. Breathing deeply of the pure air, climb higher and higher. Savor the scent of the trees; feel the peaceful solitude; hear the birds and other sounds of nature.

You feel a growing sense of expectancy. This feeling intensifies as you approach the top of the mountain. There the music will help reveal something important for you. Allow your feelings to emerge and be expressed.

When you feel your experience on the mountaintop is complete, return along the pathway to the meadow where you began. Recollect the images and feelings you had during the experience, then open your eyes and return to your ordinary consciousness.

Exercise: The Brook

Musical suggestions:

Beethoven, Symphony #9, 3rd movement
Respighi, Pines of Rome, "Gianicola"
Smetana, Moldau (to ocean)
Jethro Tull, Stand Up, "Bouree"

Return to the meadow you have learned to visualize. It is a landscape now familiar to your inner mind. But now as you look around, you will see a brook. Look at the water and the banks; note the details.

When you have looked at the brook long enough, you may want to explore it further. You may want to go upstream, following the brook to its source. Or you may want to follow the flow downstream, watching the brook grow to be a river as it moves toward the ocean. Let the music take you wherever it wants.

Whether you go to the source or to the ocean, explore your feelings as you trace the pathway of your brook. When you reach the end of the journey, spend time there savoring your feelings and images. They may not be images of the brook, but memories or emotions that arise from the experience of moving with the brook.

When you are ready, make your way back to the meadow where you began. When you have reviewed and integrated your experiences, open your eyes and find yourself in your room.

Exercise: The House

Musical suggestions:

Bach: Brandenburg Concertos
Guitar music is very effective here.
Bach, "Sarabande"
Mozart: Concerto for Flute and Harp *(Marcel Grandjany, Harp)*
Rodrigo, Concierto de Aravijuez, *Adagio*
Vivaldi, Concerto in D, *Adante*

You are in the familiar meadow again, but this time you notice something which had escaped your attention on the previous occasions. It is a house surrounded by a small, well-kept garden. It looks friendly, inviting. Look at the house, notice its details —the roof, the color of the walls, the style of the windows, the scent of the shrubbery.

You walk toward the house. Allow yourself to recognize your feelings as you approach the front door. As you come closer, stop and look at the house, and notice each detail.

Perhaps you would like to change some of the details so that they are more to your liking. You will be able to change them effortlessly. When you have remodeled the outside to your liking, open the front door and walk in.

Enter each room in turn and notice the effect it has on you. Here, too, you may redecorate as you please. Note your own change of feelings as you effect each successive change in the rooms.

Finally, fill your house with the people you would want to have live in it. Make it perfect in every respect.

When you have achieved your ideal house, return to the meadow, and then re-enter your ordinary consciousness in your ordinary surroundings.

Exercise: A Friend

Musical suggestions:
Debussy, Dances Sacred and Profane
Delius, In a Summer Garden
Moody Blues, Days of Future Past, "Knights in White Satin"
Ravel, Introduction and Allegro
V. Williams, "Fantasia on Greensleeves"

As the music begins, you find yourself once again in the familiar meadow. So many different things have happened here, that you are not surprised to find someone walking toward you. This someone may be a man, a woman, a child, an animal, a bird, or a spirit. The music will tell you which it is.

As you move toward one another, you notice gestures of openness and invitation. Immediately you feel that you could become very friendly with this someone. When you are close together, look deeply at this someone and allow your feelings to emerge. With this someone you could learn to share your deepest thoughts. You know there would be a total understanding. Perhaps you speak to each other; perhaps your communication is nonverbal. Allow a closeness and friendly intimacy to develop.

Perhaps the music will suggest you walk together through the meadow. Watch how your new friend moves. Notice his behavior and reactions. Find ways to allow the friendship to deepen.

When you return to the meadow and part from your new friend, know that you can return to this friend on subsequent trips. Collect your thoughts and happy feelings, and return to ordinary consciousness.

Exercise: On a Raft

Musical suggestions:

Brahms, Symphony #3, 3rd movement
Brahms, Symphony #1, 3rd movement
Debussy, Prelude to Afternoon of a Faun
N. Luboff choir, Inspiration, "Deep River"

Return to the meadow which is now very familiar to you, and find again the stream which you once explored. Construct a raft for yourself, for the music is to take you on a journey on the river. Fashion the raft in such a way that it will contain everything you will need as you travel. You may even want to give it a name.

The music may suggest feelings of adventure and excitement and you may want to investigate here and there along the way—something that attracts you on the shore, something deep in the water, another boat nearby.

The music may invite you into a mood of peace and tranquility and you will be content to enjoy the water and the journey in a relaxed manner. Note the people, places, and events you encounter along the way.

When you feel satisfied, make your way back to the meadow, then open your eyes and find yourself in ordinary consciousness.

Exercise: The Ocean

Musical suggestions:

Debussy, La Mer, *Part I*
Elgar, Enigma Variations, *#8, #9*
The Ultimate Seashore *(a recording of ocean sounds)*
Respighi, Pines of Rome, *"Appian Way"*

If you enjoy beginning your experience in the meadow, go there. But the music will call you to the sea. Let the music take you there.

Find a place by the ocean where you can see the water and hear the waves as they sweep the shore, where you can feel the sand, the wind, and the sun. It may be a hidden place, or along the open coast.

Immerse yourself in the depth and immensity of the scene. Explore your feelings quietly, as you remain in the presence of these great manifestations of natural power. Let the music bring out your deepest feelings in this setting.

When you have reached and enjoyed a deep level of peace and tranquility, return to ordinary consciousness.

Exercise: The Source of Energy

Musical suggestions:

Bach, Toccata and Fuque in D
Miles Davis, In a Silent Way
Mahavishnu, My Goals Beyond, *Side 2*
Tony Scott, Music for Zen Meditation
Stravinsky, Firebird Suite *(last 10 min. of record)*

Let the music take you inside your body. You are on a search for the source of your energy. Try to find the well-springs of your power and strength—that which enables you to move, walk, talk, work, dance; that which enables you to think, remember, hope, love.

Let the music suggest how you are structured and integrated, how to best use the energies at your disposal, how to realize their true potential. Focus your body on its center of power and life. Linger there, enjoying the knowledge of endless resources, in contact with the inexhaustible power of nature.

The music will suggest ways in which you can utilize your new self-understanding in daily life.

When the experience has achieved a fullness and reached completion, return to normal consciousness.

Mood Exercises

The following three exercises apply the mood *iso-principle* (see chapter 2) and focus on images directly related to the music. If your feelings are positive, buoyant, and satisfying, find musical selections (see list in appendix) that match your mood. In this way, your mood will be reinforced and strengthened.

If your mood is negative and unsatisfying, begin with a selection that matches your mood without reinforcing it, able to turn it in a more positive direction. When your mood has taken an upswing, change to a musical selection with a positive mood—joy, peace, unity, excitement—and let the music absorb you into this.

Exercise: The Peace Composer

(Although the title of this exercise suggests the theme of peace, you may select music which matches either your present mood or some feeling you wish to reinforce—for example, love, joy, energy, unity, or excitement.)

Allow the music to fill your body, as though your skin held the sound inside it. Let it flow irresistibly into your ears; let it descend through your throat into your chest and trunk, into your arms and down through your legs. Let the shape and patterns and color of the music adopt the contours and textures of your body. Feel your body as it takes the rhythm and tempo of the sound into itself.

As the music continues to flow down into you, your skin may begin to tingle. Let it resonate to the music's energy. Savor this sensation. Allow the music to touch your emotions and feelings.

Slowly and gradually, you fill to overflowing with music. The tingling of your skin grows more intense. First, perhaps, at the tips of your fingers you begin to feel the music pass out from your body into the room, as if your fingertips had themselves become composers transmitting the music.

Soon, you feel that not only your fingers but your hands and arms are exuding music; then your feet and your legs. Finally, your whole body, from marrow to skin, begins to transform the music. Listen to the new music coming from you. Feel its rhythms, its pulse, its melody.

Your whole body pours out music—music akin to the music you hear yet your own music. You are its author. You are transforming what is entering you, and it emerges as an expression of your own inner self. Enjoy the freedom of this self-expression.

Exercise: The Musical Performer

Somewhere in the levels of your consciousness, there is a space where you are a performer. It is a place where all your ordinary inhibitions are forgotten, where your manual dexterity is at its highest, where your deepest feelings are free to express themselves in music. This is the place—the performance space—which is explored here. Instrumental or vocal solo selections are the best musical choices for this exercise.

As you listen to the music, let its mood penetrate you. Allow your whole body to feel it. Your aim is to enjoy the experience of performing this piece yourself—in your imagination.

You must feel the music deeply. The entire body should participate if the performance is to be satisfying and.effective. Deep inside you is where the music begins. Its mood and feeling should bubble out naturally, freely, like an underground spring. Allow time for the music to fill you. Let it course throughout your body so that every limb knows it and resonates in empathy with its mood. You want all of you to take part in this performance.

See the hands of the performer playing the piece. Watch their movement. Observe their gracefulness, their confidence, their accuracy and speed. Notice how each finger is poised to express the feelings it holds within itself.

Now, slowly, see your own hands and fingers taking over those of the performer. Let your fingers move with the same dexterity as his. Feel your own finger-tips, how they tingle with excitement, eager to touch the instrument, poised to express the music sensed within them.

Once you can see yourself at ease while perform-ing, simply relax and enjoy the experience. Your body will play effortlessly and perfectly.

When the piece ends, or when the experience has satisfied you, bring yourself back to ordinary con-sciousness with a three-two-one count, reminding yourself that you will remember how to return to your performance space whenever you wish.

Exercise: The Responsive Instrument

Just as the musician must contribute the proper mood and intensity to any performance, so the in-strument must be responsive to the performer. Only when performer and instrument work together is true music created. Another possible experience, there-fore, for the listener in altered consciousness is to identify with the instrument(s) played by the soloist or orchestra.

Choose music that relates to the mood you wish to express. As it plays, let its mood slowly work its way into you. Imagine the melody and movement of the music entering your heart: Let it be pumped into your body through your arteries and veins. Watch the mood and rhythm of the music fill your blood-stream. As the arteries deep in the body send their content into the capillaries on the surface of the skin, and the sensitive skin begins to respond with tingling reactions, you know that the instrument is ready to respond to the performer.

Imagine yourself physically turning into the instrument you wish to become. Perhaps you wish to be the keyboard of a piano, the strings of a guitar, the bow of a violin, the bell of a trumpet. The music will suggest what is most appropriate for you.

It may take a few moments to become accustomed to your new role as instrument, so give your body–mind plenty of time to feel at home in its new role. Enjoy the feeling of performing as an instrument, totally cooperating with the performer. This is a very deep sharing space, especially if you can relate through feelings to your performer.

When the piece is completed, return to your normal consciousness.

With practice, you may be able to assume both roles—performer and instrument—while in altered states of consciousness. And, as you will have realized by now, you are really the composer of this experience. Thus you can become simultaneously composer, performer, and instrument.

Chapter 4

Listening in a Group

The experiences and techniques described in the previous chapters are for listening to music as an *individual* in an altered state of consciousness. If this changed consciousness is induced in a *group* session, new dimensions can be opened up in the listening experience. What follows are accounts of the experiences of groups, from different professional and social backgrounds, who have used the new way to music.

Mantra

Mantra is a drug rehabilitation center in Baltimore. A demonstration of the new way to music was arranged with some of the staff there. They are professionally familiar with psychedelic experiences and with drug usage in young people. The atmosphere of their center is relaxed and informal.

Each induction should be adapted to the needs of a particular group at a particular time. Since the people at Mantra were extremely imaginative and experienced, a more "far out" induction procedure was designed than might be used with an ordinary group. The group was familiar with rock music, so the program included both classic and rock, exploring sounds from Cat Stevens' *Morning Has Broken* to

Respighi's *Pines of Rome*. What follows is the induction used:

Let yourself down in the chair with all your weight. Loosen your belts, take off your shoes, take off your glasses. There may be noises around but these will not be important if you concentrate on my voice. When my voice stops, transfer your attention to the music, so that your attention will always be either on my voice or on the music.

Now think of relaxation: Relax the body, relax the mind, particularly; will to go into the experience, no matter what comes. The first thing we will do is the relaxation exercise. (That noise outside the door is the man cleaning the floors. If you concentrate on my voice, the noise will not bother you.)

To help you with the relaxation, it is a good idea to think of the aura which, as experiments have now demonstrated, apparently covers the entire body. It is an energy field, two to three inches wide, which emerges from the skin. Some people can actually see these energy fields with the naked eye. So I'd like you to think of this aura surrounding your body, and I'd like you to extend its width from two or three inches to five or six inches. Feel this added energy circling your body. It is available to send its energy back into your body. And as the energy enters your body it causes a great relaxation, so that the body may reach its most comfortable state.

Now, think of this energy field around you, pulsating with life, the kind of energy that is relaxing, making you feel at home with yourself. Visualize this energy coming through the top of your head or flowing around the scalp. And as this energy flows, you feel the relaxation entering each cell of the skin of the scalp, and coming over the fore-head and relaxing the eyes, so that the eyelids feel very heavy and the eyes feel at rest. Just completely relaxed.

Now you have this feeling also over your nose and over your cheekbones, and down in your throat and in your mouth. You are so relaxed that your tongue feels heavy in your mouth. These waves of relaxation come one after another over your head and scalp, over your eyes, so that your eyelids feel very heavy. It's a very good feeling; it's a very relaxing feeling. And for some it's a very warm, comfortable feeling as well.

Let this relaxation come down the back of your head and down around and through the muscles of the neck, in the sinews, relaxing each part, each cell in the neck. And as the muscles of the neck relax, the muscles of the shoulders relax, and the skin that surrounds the neck relaxes. If you feel any tenseness, just move your neck and shoulders a little bit until you feel more comfortable.

Allow this relaxation to continue over the shoulders to the upper arms, and to the lower arms, coming down and relaxing not only the skin but going into the arm itself and relaxing the muscles there, into the flow of the blood, into the bone itself, so that every part of the body is in perfect harmony. It is flowing down over the shoulders into the upper arms, the lower arms, and through the fingers. And as this flow comes down, your arms feel heavy and warm. The flow of relaxation comes down to the spine, down through the neck into the spine, so that you feel relaxation around each of the vertebrae and in all the muscles that extend from the spine. You feel this wonderful

*sense of warmth and heaviness, and at the same
time it is a lightness, as this energy courses
through the body. It comes through into the trunk
area, into each cell of the lungs, so that the breathing becomes low and quiet. You feel that all is
well. Let it go down into the stomach and the vis-
ceral areas of the body, and down through the
trunk, feeling very heavy and warm. Now down
through the legs, the thighs, into the knees and the
calves, and down to the feet and the toes.*

*Feel wave upon wave of this relaxation pouring
over your body. If there are any places in the body
that are still unrelaxed, move them a little bit and
get them into a comfortable position. Now sink
down into the chair so that the body is so relaxed,
so well taken care of, that you no longer have to
pay any attention to it.*

*It is there; it is fine. And now that the mind is free,
the imagination can proceed into whatever experience is in store for you.*

The Exercise at Mantra

When the group members had achieved deep relaxation, the listening exercise began. The countdown
followed a normal pattern, from one to ten. The
meadow setting was used and the musical program
began with Cat Stevens' resurrection song, "Morning Has Broken," followed by Delius' *In a Summer
Garden.* After the Delius piece, the music was interrupted and the group was asked to come back to the
meadow. They were given a choice: to go up the
stream or down the stream. They were told: "No
matter which direction you choose, you will soon
come to a lovely pool hidden in the trees, and there
is a beautiful waterfall splashing into the pool." Then

the "Gianicola" suite from Respighi's *Pines of Rome* was played.

The music was interrupted again. The directions were to gather at the river to get on a boat that takes everyone down to the ocean. Note that each individual had the opportunity to depict the scene in his own way. They were not told, for example, that everyone was together on the bank, or that they were all in the same boat. It was not specified whether people were sitting or standing, silent or talking, happy or sad. All this was left to the individual imagination. For this setting, "Bouree" from Jethro Tull's rock album *Stand Up* was used.

After "Bouree," the directions continued: "We get off the boat now and stand on the beach." This was followed by a recording of ocean waves crashing against the sand, titled "The Ultimate Seashore." In this last experience there were no sounds but those of the ocean.

The exercise was concluded with a ten-to-one count-out, and the discussion began.

The Discussion

One participant had trouble getting into the experience. "Everytime I would sink down into the experience," he explained, "I would get uncomfortable. This chair I'm sitting on is not good for that experience." Many commented on the importance of feeling relaxed and comfortable if the listening experience is to succeed.

One subject described his experiences from the meadow to the waterfall. "I really didn't like *In a Summer Garden*. At first it sounded so serene and quiet, I had a sense of false serenity—nature just isn't that way—and knew that something was going to have to change. And soon it got really violent. A hawk chased a rabbit and finally caught it. After that, some butterflies were being chased, but they escaped."

His experiences were full of flying objects. "I saw lots of birds through the whole thing—some mystical ones, too, flying with other birds . . . First it was swans, then it changed to a young girl. I had this impression that there were young birds that had never flown before and they were flying higher and higher until they reached a peak, and then they flew off. It reminded me of the "Brewster McCloud" flying scene—being millions of miles up, looking down at the lake and just floating. I flew all the way up the stream."

The heart at the center of the universe with every throb hurls the flood of happiness into every artery, vein and veinlet, so that the whole system is inundated with tides of joy. The plenty of the poorest place is too great; the harvest cannot be gathered. Every sound ends in music. The edge of every surface is tinged with prismatic rays.

Ralph Waldo Emerson

Once the discussion reached the boatride to the ocean (Jethro Tull's music), the participants had many comments. One man said he liked going in the boat. Another had a negative reaction. "That terrified me," he said. "There were heavy sounds of breathing, and everything about it frightened me. There were too many people around."

The Jethro Tull music does, in fact, include heavy breathing sounds. In normal listening, we don't react adversely to these sounds, but in a heightened consciousness their inappropriateness on the recording is magnified.

A third participant turned the boatride into a party. "I liked it," he said. "We were having lots of fun at a party. We were sitting on the edge of the boat kicking our feet in the water, having fun. Then someone pushed me in. I broke part of the slab and tried to get into the boat again. By then it was time to go to the seashore music, so I don't know if I got back on the boat or not."

The experience in general, they admitted, resembled a drug experience. 'The places we got into when listening today," said one, "are pretty much the same as those via drug experience, but the music is not at all as demanding." Many felt that the experience became more engrossing as it continued. "When you started the ocean ("The Ultimate Seashore"),'' said one man, "I didn't recognize it for a bit. Then, when I recognized it, I was really surprised. I really thought it was an ocean there. It was really great. Probably the closest to being away. After a while, I didn't even hear the ocean. I didn't hear anything."

Listening At Home

The participants in the Mantra demonstration were therapists and counsellors with a professional interest in the techniques of this new use of music. Some of the most satisfying listening experiences can take place with a group of friends gathered in one's own home. The account that follows is of one such experience.

Four women friends participated in an evening listening session. Helen and Dee, secretaries in their late forties, work together; Ann is a nurse in her mid-thirties; Helen's daughter, Gail, just home from college, was the fourth.

They were already acquainted with the concept of listening with altered consciousness and arrived for the session with strong, positive expectations.

Dee

Dee suspected that she would not be able to relax sufficiently to fully experience a heightened consciousness. The suggestion to find a meadow and a stream was not particularly satisfying for her, so she imagined herself on the seashore where she felt more relaxed.

"I wandered along the beach. The sky, ocean and sand seemed to blend into a single backdrop. There was no one on the beach, and I thought of how much my dog Charlie would like it there, too. He became part of the scene, and we played together. I felt myself wanting to participate more fully," she said, "thinking I was not letting myself go enough. I think now that I would have relaxed more if I had not been trying so hard. Yet, when it was suggested that we come back, I was very unwilling. I think I realized *then* that I had been more relaxed than I thought. I wanted to lose myself, or hide, so that I wouldn't hear the voice telling us to come back."

Like many others entering altered consciousness for the first time, Dee wondered as she began discussing her experience with the others whether she had experienced anything different from ordinary consciousness. "When I started to talk about my experiences," she said later, "I realized that they *were* experiences and not just something I had forced myself to create in fantasy."

Gail

An art student, Gail is used to visualizing and admits to being an experienced daydreamer. "But my daydreams are never as beautiful as this," was her comment on the new listening experience.

To underline the depth of her relaxation, Gail explained that she can't usually lie on her back. "I can't believe that I was on my back for forty-five minutes and didn't move a muscle!"

During their fantasies, three of the women remained *alone*. Gail was the only one to visualize other people, and, even for her, others appeared only twice in the entire program. Once, she walked along a stream with her boyfriend. "Nothing was said. We both simply strolled along enjoying the beauty around us." Later she saw her father (recently deceased) seated in heaven surrounded by "angels in long white robes."

Ann

In the discussion Ann raised a question about negative experiences. "What happens when you go into a space that you don't like?"

It was explained that in such a case the listener can do a number of things: The mind may create confusing images, sending out a kind of static interference to lessen the impact of the negative material. Or it may simply shut itself off in the face of threatening images and the individual goes to sleep. Usually, however, if the person is willing to confront the experience, the unconscious will generate a solution to the problem. Ann's unconscious selected the third technique.

As a child, she had lived in a home near the ocean. She remembered it as filled with unhappy memories. When the guide suggested visualizing a stream, Ann was whisked in her fantasy to the ocean. When she turned around to look away from the sea, she saw her former home. It brought back negative feelings. She definitely did not want to be there, and at this point her creative unconscious took over:

> *Out of the ground sprouted a giant green stalk with a fantastic pink flower. Many years ago I had dreamed about this flower in exactly the same spot, and now I was visualizing it again. I sat on the petals of the flower and it lifted me up to a cloud—with a steering wheel! As soon as I realized that I and my cloud were leaving the scene, I felt comfortable and relaxed, thinking things are not always what they seem.*

At the close of the session, Ann experienced a "struggle to get back into normal focus. I felt very far away during the discussion afterwards," she said.

Helen

As a result of the listening experiment, Helen discovered she had a natural ability to achieve new levels of consciousness. "I never imagined an altered state of consciousness could be so deep and beautiful," was her summary of the experience. Through the music selections she experienced a pleasant floating or soaring sensation, like a bird in flight.

People often feel a sense of lightness or imagine themselves moving their hands or dancing. Helen's arms actually rose involuntarily from the couch on which she was lying. She became aware of the movement during the experience and lowered her arms. At least three or four times during the program her arms lifted involuntarily.

At this stage, the listener loses his sense of reality. The sounds of music are felt as coming, not only from the outside, but also from his own emotions ... such an experience induces an "oceanic feeling" which is joined by a feeling of magical omnipotence and a return to a primitive kinaesthetic pleasure, as if the listener were flying through the universe on the wings of sound.

H. Kohut and S. Levarie

During the Tschesnokoff selection, "Salvation is Created," Helen had a quiet peak experience which might be called "religious."

"As the voices crossed my conciousness," she said, "I was transported to a huge cathedral. There was no one in the church, nor was I even aware of a choir— just emptiness and the beautiful voices filling everything everywhere in the church."

While returning to normal consciousness, the four women had been told that they would remember the new spaces they had captured in their minds, and would remember how to travel there again. Helen was the only one who reported trying to re-enter this new space in her consciousness. It happened some days after the first experience. Her report is as follows:

Yesterday, while lunching on our patio, I became aware of the chattering birds feeding their young in the birdhouses above me. As I finished my lunch, I felt surrounded by their sounds, which I found most pleasant. I stretched out on the chaise lounge, and counted myself down as the guide had done.
I felt a surge of relaxation, and was transported to a lovely forest. I became part of the world of the birds, which in this scene was deep in the forest, with towering trees all around. As I floated along with the sounds of the birds, I became aware of an opening at the top of the giant trees. It was a small patch of sun-drenched sky and I wanted to float through that opening into the sky above. I felt my arms and hands lifting as though I were soaring. Although perfectly content in this relaxed experience, I decided to come out of it, as my daughter was present and we had things to do. She said my arms remained raised for a few minutes. The experience was not nearly as long as that two evenings before, but it probably could have lasted longer had I so desired.
Normally, after lunch, I feel sleepy and find it an effort to resume activities. But as I returned to normal consciousness, I felt completely rested and renewed in energy.

Helen is a natural subject for altered states of consciousness. After one experience, she had learned to relax and to self-induce a heightened consciousness, finding enough music simply in the sounds of the birds.

There are sounds around you right now. Listen to them. Ordinarily you do not notice them because the brain has blocked them out. It is only when you concentrate on listening **that you become aware of these environmental sounds.**

             Lawrence Eisman

The involuntary rising of Helen's arms while in altered consciousness is not unusual. The phenomenon is called *ideomotor activity*, meaning that the motor activity is controlled by unconscious ideational thought.

An Experiment with College Women

A psychology professor at a private women's college was approached with the suggestion that she explore the new way to music with an informal group of students. She agreed and helped design a forty-five minute listening tape. Its theme was nature; its objective, "searching for the source." Some of her suggestions for visual settings were adapted from Leuner's paper on guided affective imagery. The settings and corresponding musical selections for her experiment are as follows:

Meadow scene: Ravel, Daphnis and Chloe (beginning)
Along the stream: Brahms, Symphony #1 in C (3rd movement)
At the pond: Debussy, Girl with the Flaxen Hair
      Respighi, The Pines of Rome, *"Gianicola"*
Searching for the source: Debussy, Sirenes, "Nocturne"
At the source: Tschesnokoff, "Salvation is Created"
Coming back: Scott, Lotus Land

This listening program was scheduled for four different nights in a small recreation room. Pillows and mattresses were spread on the floor. There was a loudspeaker in each corner of the room. About half a dozen students agreed to come on each occasion. Some came expecting to be hypnotized. Others thought the experience was going to bring back deep memories. A few had vague fears of losing control, flipping out, of being used as guinea pigs, of being asked to discuss very personal feelings. One girl said, "I figured either nothing would happen, or something very strange." (She later described her experiences as "very, very strange.")

The professor first explained the theory of listening to music in altered states of consciousness, and then outlined the procedure of relaxation, induction, listening, and return to normal consciousness.

The experimenter was able to deal with most of the anxieties and misconceptions before beginning the program. Each girl had been asked to bring a blindfold to facilitate concentration, and most of them found it helpful. Those that did not, removed their blindfolds. Students were asked to remove their shoes, glasses, and other potential sources of annoyance or discomfort, and to lie comfortably on their backs. The experimenter used a traditional muscle stretching and relaxing technique, working upward from the toes to the head. The relaxation, which took about ten minutes, was followed by an induction procedure. She suggested that the students visualize a stairway leading to a meadow. The countdown, from ten to zero, carried them down the stairs and into non-ordinary levels of consciousness.

Between selections, the experimenter made very brief suggestions to the effect that the students were

now along a stream, now at the pond, now nearing
the source, and so on, through the rest of the settings.
Before the Debussy *Sirenes*, a second countdown was
given to help subjects deepen their trance.

Some of the students found the interim suggestions and second countdown helpful, others didn't.
Many found themselves far from the suggested ponds
and meadows. These usually remained wherever they
were, wherever the music was leading them—following the initial instruction given to them.

Mary Ann

Mary Ann is a college freshman, majoring in eco-
nomics. She prefers listening to rock and romantic
music, and is a fan of big band sounds from Glen
Miller to Henry Mancini.

She came to the group listening session expecting
"to experience something totally new and somewhat
mysterious." Her only fear was that she "wouldn't
be able to participate correctly." She had done relaxing exercises before, and, in fact, often used them to
help put herself to sleep at night.

During the induction, the guide suggested that the
individuals descend a staircase leading to a meadow.
Mary Ann had no difficulty visualizing this. She described her mood and feelings during the first four
pieces as content, satisfied, joyful, exhilarated. Here
is her account of her experiences:

*By the time I was in the meadow, I was completely
relaxed and content. I felt as if I had jumped down
from the last step into the meadow. The jump
lasted for quite a while; it was almost a floating
feeling. When I landed, I was in a meadow with*

golden brown wheat fields and green pasture land. When we were told to move on, I walked toward the brook. Before then, however, I was jumping all around.

In this part of the trip, I really began to feel as if I was floating and soaring through the air like a bird. Suddenly, I plunged into the blue water. I was back in my body again. I wasn't dressed, however. I was swimming in the nude, mostly under water, not even worrying about breathing. I was swimming with someone else. Thoroughly relaxed and happy, I was looking at all the underwater plants, fish and animals. Then I swam up and up and around.

I guess this part was the best part of the pond. I was free and sort of slinky like an eel in the water. When the guide told us to seek the source, I was somewhat disappointed and mad at having to leave this part.

I felt as if I were chopping down dense brush to get through. I was frustrated at times because it seemed very difficult to chop down the brush and to fight my way through. I felt as if I were climbing a long, rocky mountain. It reminded me of a mountain climb I took two years ago in Austria. It was tough, but very rewarding at the top.

The additional countdown relaxed me more and more deeply.

I was very satisfied here. There were feelings of love. I felt as if I were on the borderline between heaven and earth. This image of heaven probably reflects the image I received in grade school. The sky was the most beautiful blue color I have ever seen, there were numerous birds flying around, and the clouds were majestic, tremendous—beautifully *fluffy and soft-looking.*

I was very angry when I heard the leader's voice telling me I had to come back. I didn't want to leave. I was afraid to come back into the troubled world. It was really fantastic to be at the source of the brook.

As I was walking back, and at times running, I saw a gypsy wagon and gypsies—I guess due to the prevalence of the tambourine in the music. I just kept moving on until I was gradually coming back into reality. I found that I was able to move quite easily again.

When Mary Ann returned to normal consciousness, she felt groggy for a few minutes, trying to put everything together. She was very relaxed and at ease during the discussion and expressed surprise at her experience, surprise "that I was successful in taking the trip."

When asked about her specifically physical reactions, she replied that it had been very difficult to move at times. "At one point," she explained, "I had to scratch but couldn't." (The guide should remember to tell listeners in altered states of consciousness that they will be able to move their hands, feet, or body whenever necessary. Like many others, Mary Ann felt she needed the guide's "permission" to move in any way.)

In a programmatic composition, it is not always possible to know exactly what the composer is describing just by listening to the music. Program music may stimulate the imagination, but unless the composer explains the extra-musical meaning of his work it is

almost certain that each listener will imagine something quite different.

Lawrence Eisman

Andrea

Andrea, an enthusiastic college freshman, had embarked on the listening program with some apprehension, afraid that she might somehow lose control. But she grew more comfortable when she recognized some of her friends in the room, and had no trouble relaxing or entering altered consciousness. Her experiences were quite consistent throughout—feelings of love and affection in response to the music.

I was standing in a green field and saw myself in a long, yellow chiffon gown, flowing ecstatically in the wind. A fantastically beautiful black stallion came cantering towards me, and stopped for me to mount. The wind was the dominant impression. In my fantasy I had very long and loose hair, and it was trailing behind me as I rode the stallion.

While I was riding along—and the music swelled —I was met by another black stallion with a very handsome and gallant gentleman as his rider. He accompanied me in my ride, and I had a feeling we were both escaping from something. We stopped by a pond and sat down. We stared at each other's reflections and communicated in this way. I had a sense of total understanding and compassion.

With the music, my emotion was transfixed. If

*the music swelled, so did my heart. Whatever
emotion I was going through intensified along with
the music.*

*My companion and I returned to a dark castle.
There was an immediate sense of fear and depres-
sion. For some reason, he was not supposed to be
there, and he couldn't let himself get caught with
me. I felt as though I was running out of time, and
a very dark, somber mood settled on me. My experience had come to an end and I accepted it. My
companion left me, and I watched his figure disappearing into nothingness.*

On returning to ordinary consciousness Andrea
felt contented, "with a little sadness mixed in." Like
most of her friends, she was surprised at the experience, eager to repeat it, and anxious to share
her adventures.

Marty

A biology major, Marty is an intense young
woman, who at the age of eighteen had already completed her sophomore year. She had been taking piano
lessons for three years and listened to music "every
chance I get." Her taste in music is as broad as her
enthusiasm for it—from James Taylor to Wagner,
Simon & Garfunkel to Liszt, The Who to Bizet, Bob
Dylan to Beethoven.

At first, it seemed as if she might not respond
well to altered states of consciousness. She arrived
appearing anxious, and, later, admitted feeling this
way. She was afraid of the other people in the group,
and shy about doing the physical relaxation exercises. "They made me too conscious of my body."
She resented the guide's voice, found that it "was

made too sweet." Two things helped: wearing a blindfold and finding a close friend among the participants.

Then the music—Ravel's *Daphnis and Chloe*—took over. Here are her reactions:

Couldn't get into a meadow, as suggested. Went to ocean instead, feeling relaxed and contented. Swam underwater and took a ride on a sea turtle. Swam freely with other animals in sea. Then became conscious of world above. Went up there, flew around in air. Became lonely for life that was in sea. Went back down and brought sea creatures up into the air.

Took walk on beach, very conscious of my footsteps. Was completely naked and enjoying it immensely. Cut my hair—was taking too long to dry. I wasn't worried about any incongruity in this dream. Was enjoying all the fantastic experiences. Enjoyed music, but was constantly waiting for the big climax. Never came. Was always conscious of crashing of waves. Water was extremely clear.

Brahms: Symphony #1 in C, 3rd movement

Don't remember too much about music. Concentrated on visual experiences. Can't really say if they were stimulated by music. I knew what I was feeling and was enjoying it. Music was backing up that mood, so everything was fine. Was conscious again of noise stream was making. Saw myself gracefully dancing along side of stream. Remembered banks of stream—saw how grass and roots grew out of the earth. Never spoke, but my face was very expressive. No incongruities in this scene. Could hardly wait to move on—found my-self jumping ahead of suggestions.

Debussy: *Girl With the Flaxen Hair*

Didn't like music—too sweet. Explored pond. Found deer and rabbits. Ran away. Mostly had fantasies looking into water and imagining things.

Respighi: *The Pines of Rome*

Was glad you suggested fountain. Love fountains. Had dozens of fountains. Ran in between them, through them, over them. Had a blast! Jumped on top of one and it carried me up to the sky, like you see happen in cartoons. I was playful, frolic-some, elated.

Debussy: *Sirenes "Nocturne"*

Very conscious of music—didn't need additional countdown—was very into what I was doing. Wanted to swim in water, but was conscious of current flowing against me. Was not a pastoral stream, but had barren, rocky banks. Don't re-member how I moved—at times I remember run-ning. Saw goats.
Was not fearful, but anxious. Realized that at any minute I might not like what would happen. Had a feeling of supernatural presence in the rest of the world. Became heavier, did not want the rest of world with me. Realized its presence was there only to hinder me, and I refused to be hindered. Ignored the feeling. Was too determined to find the source. Had a feeling of revelation coming up soon.

Tschesnokoff: *Salvation is Created*

Came to source. Was chilly—wanted to shiver but couldn't. Melting snow was creating a stream. Snow was glowing blue and dripping from a rocky ledge. Found blanket and laid down to get warm.

Woke up in a huge cathedral. Walked up the main aisle and met Jesus at the altar. Knew some revelation was about to come. Jesus spoke only through his eyes. They were deep and sad but had acceptance and understanding in them. He took me to hill overlooking the Roman Forum and displayed all the ruins to me with his hand.

He looked deep into me. I did not avoid the penetrating eyes, even though I knew he might not like what he saw.

I looked away and saw three crosses on a hill. I grabbed Jesus' hand. He smiled and showed me who was on the cross. I knew the person and felt sadness and tragedy, but accepted the fact.

Felt inner peace, but was suffering. Did not fight suffering. Accepted it. Dropped Jesus' hand. Was standing below three crosses looking up at gray sky. Jesus was no longer present bodily, but I could feel what he had left.

Music inspired mood at first, but then I forgot about music. Mood took over. Atmosphere was gloomy, dark, and gray. Sky was prevalent. It was a beautiful, sad sky.

Scott: Lotus Land

Music took over here. Was feeling extremely satisfied and deeply human, but music made me move on. Began walking down steps into ancient city. Was very conscious of white walls of building. Everything was stone. Music was penetrating further and I went with it.

I heard you telling me to come back, but the music did not suggest it. I didn't want to go back to the pool and water. Felt I was past these.

I walked through city and came to an open door. Walked in. Was conscious of smoky interior—it glowed red. People were there but I could not see them or associate with them. They didn't seem to notice my entrance.

Heard clinking noise and saw glimpse of belly dancer. I lay down on cushions and breathed in smoke; it had a pleasant smell. I accepted everything and everyone in room. Felt I knew them and understood. Didn't speak to anyone, but could feel their moods. Felt many different moods, but accepted them all. Felt ashamed of nothing. There was a freedom in accepting all these people.

I enjoyed this music so much more than previous selections. It was mysterious and deep—no frills. It caught me and carried me with it.

Could not come back to reality—was not conscious of the experience ever ending. Your voice finally broke in and I knew I had to come back. I rose very gradually. Again, count-out didn't really help. I knew I was coming out, and I wanted to take my time.

After this intense experience, it was natural for Marty to want to return slowly to normal consciousness. She also wanted to think a while about what had happened before sharing her experiences. "Mostly," she said later, "I wanted to discuss the experiences with myself first, and then have a group session."

Marty is not a particularly religious person, yet her peak experience definitely had a religious dimension. No one would have predicted that she would meet Jesus. Consciousness does surprising things: Among a group of religious women, meditative music listening sessions generated few if any traditional religious images.

Marty's response was filled with vivid imagery and recognizable characters; other listeners experience moods more than visual fantasy. Some tend to see colors and shapes rather than people and places; still others tend to feel presences rather than to picture things. A few favor insights over feelings or moods. The new levels of consciousness accommodate all these preferences. None is better than any other. Each indicates a personal inclination, one's individual response to the new dimensions of consciousness.

At times, subjects may feel bad because they cannot visualize as well as the next person. The guide should suggest that each person seek the medium of expression most natural to his unconscious.

Summary

Most of the students came to the sessions with vague apprehensions, but then relaxed and thoroughly enjoyed the experience. A number of them described consciousness of their bodies in different ways. One said, "I didn't feel my body—only my mind and head were there." Another remarked, "Once in a while a toe or an arm or some part of my body would start feeling strange, but I tried not to let it bother me." Another felt " a heaviness in my arms—great indifference to anything going on around me." A fourth recalled that her body felt very numb. "I felt as if I had to concentrate on an arm or a leg to make sure it was still there. I was leaving my body behind as my mind went places."

Most said that external circumstances—traffic, people's voices—had not influenced them, but one of them integrated an external circumstance into her listening. "The window behind me was open, and the breeze coming through fit into my feelings of lightness."

Students of Music

Among the group of college listeners, music majors seemed to have a few special problems. The new way to music suggests that the listener allow the music to take him or her wherever it will; yet students of music are trained to analyze the music itself, and this may generate some internal conflicts and inhibit the ability to fantasize.

All the music majors who tried listening in altered states of .consciousness encountered this problem initially—especially during the Brahms' symphony, which they had recently studied in class. But eventually all were able to let go and allow the music to carry them into new states of consciousness.

Music demands an alert mind of intellectual capacity, but it is far from being an intellectual exercise. Musical cerebration as a game for its own sake may fasci-

nate a small minority of experts or specialists, but it
has no true significance unless its rhythmic patterns
and melodic designs, its harmonic tensions and expressive timbres penetrate the deepest layer of our
subconscious mind.

Aaron Copland

Chapter 5

Exercises for a Group

The Guide

When more than one individual wishes to listen to music in altered states of consciousness, there is usually need for a guide. The guide's overall responsibility is to ensure a satisfying experience for the group members. He or she will be expected to provide a comfortable, conducive setting; to choose the musical selections; to use proper voice volume, intonation, inflection, and speed of delivery; to modify techniques to meet changing situations; to be ready to deal with any unusual behavior in the listeners.

Many of these topics have already been discussed. This section summarizes the qualities desirable in a guide, and points out typical problems that may arise.

Qualities in a Guide

A guide should have personally experienced music in altered states of consciousness, so that he may fully understand the subjects' experiences and communicate adequately with them.

A guide should be mentally healthy and emotionally stable, and should be able to instill trust and confidence in the listeners.

A good guide learns to lead the listeners without dominating them or unduly interfering with their experiences.

The more a guide knows about human psychology, the better. This book does not purport to teach him what he must know of psychology to be an effective ASC guide. Rather, it presumes sufficient knowledge and experience to enable him to cope with unusual or unforeseen reactions.

No matter how much classroom training a guide may have, his real expertise will be acquired through experience. In actual involvement with groups, he will learn new techniques, discover ways to modify his inductions to suit the needs of the moment, strengthen the most effective elements in his approach. He must be alert to each such opportunity to learn from his listeners.

Problem Areas

The guide of a group induction session has considerable control over the participants. He should realize that people in altered states of consciousness will normally do only those things suggested to them. When a listener has been helped to reach a new level of consciousness, he will not normally *initiate* any new action. Although a participant can at all times refuse to follow a suggestion, he will not usually take any positive action on his own. For example, he may become uncomfortable during a session, yet not feel free to move about to relieve his discomfort, simply because this possibility was not suggested by the guide. Therefore, it is wise to tell participants during the induction that they may change position, move about whenever they wish, swallow, or scratch an itchy nose. Shoes, eyeglasses, belts, knots in hair are other common sources of physical discomfort.

Once the paticipants are comfortable, the guide

takes care to provide a satisfying relaxation procedure. Since the goal is to enable the individual listener to self-induce new levels of consciousness, the
guide will suggest that the paticipants learn the procedures well enough to reach altered states by themselves. Ideally, when a group of experienced ASC
listeners comes together for a listening session, the
guide should simply say, "Let's each of us self-induce
an altered state of consciousness. Signal me when
you are ready."

In helping a group to relax, the following points
are important.

- It takes people longer to relax when they are
  entering new levels of consciousness for the first
  time, and the guide should therefore allow plenty
  of time for the relaxation procedure.
- The more they know and trust the guide, the more
  easily and quickly participants will relax. In a
  guide's first session with a new group, the relaxation will naturally take longer than with a familiar
  group.
- When a relaxation procedure involves relaxing
  muscles, it has been found more successful to refer
  to very specific parts of the body—right toe, right
  foot, right calf, rather than simply to the right leg.
- Members of a group will show different response
  rates to the induction: Some people achieve relaxation very slowly, others more quickly. The
  guide should aim at a reasonable time for relaxation so that the slow ones don't feel rushed and
  the fast ones don't get impatient.
- Suggest that if anything should happen that would
  require the participants' awake attention, they will
  at once return to normal consciousness. This as-

surance usually allays anxiety and permits deeper relaxation.

- Suggest that they remain entirely passive—neither straining to help or resist in any way. They should simply allow the relaxation procedure to happen in them.

Some guides ask participants to bring a blindfold with them, as many people find that a blindfold helps them to relax and concentrate and so enter more fully into altered states of consciousness.

With practice, the guide learns to recognize the signs of relaxation in his listeners. He also learns to notice individuals who are having difficulty and to respond to their particular needs, while still directing his remarks to the whole group.

The guide is at the service of the participants. His suggestions are designed to help the participant go where he wants to go, not where the guide might like him to go. The participant generates the fantasies or images; the music creates the setting. The guide merely facilitates both. He can also hinder both.

Safeguards for the Guide

The following list of built-in safeguards for the amateur guide have been compiled from experience in many practice sessions and discussions.

- Altered states of consciousness are in no way as dangerous as drug-induced states may be. It is reassuring for a guide to know that the force he is dealing with, although powerful, is not uncontrollable.
- An individual who distrusts the guide will normally not persist in the ASC experience. Do not try inducing an ASC in anyone who seems overtly reluctant or afraid.

- The choice of musical selections is important. Provide music with positive mood and feeling. Use nothing that might engender fear or anxiety. Avoid selections with many crescendos or loud cymbal crashes.
- Persons with particular interests or difficulties may wish to resolve these while in altered consciousness; the guide should, therefore, be flexible and permissive.
- Always remember that the subject is very vulnerable while in ASC, and act accordingly. Do not induce an ASC in persons under psychiatric care, unless the therapist approves.

The Discussion

Make sure that all participants return to normal consciousness. Those in deep states may need to be counted back a second or even third time. In some cases, the transition to normal consciousness is helped by providing appropriate music—selections with a light *beat*—at the end of the listening program.

Everyone should feel relaxed and refreshed when they have returned. Anyone who does not experience a pleasant return—someone who mentions a headache, for example—should be counted back a second time.

A common reaction of subjects following a listening experience in altered consciousness is that they had had a totally different experience from anything they had felt before. Normally, people do not discuss or analyze the music itself, since the music merely provided a background for their experience.

During the discussion, the guide should encourage subjects to present emotional or personal insights. If individuals expose too much of their inner feelings, the guide should gently redirect the discussion. Embarrassing or intimate self-revelations are out of place in this context, and are best reserved for sessions with a professional therapist. When such material arises, the guide should quietly make a neutral comment and let the matter drop.

Some subjects feel badly when they see that others have a more complete experience than they. The guide should explain that some people are naturally better at producing fantasies than others, and that practice will result in more rewarding experiences.

A few subjects may fall asleep during the music and deny this vigorously upon awakening. Simply let such people join in the discussion. One college girl who fell asleep during the music presented her dream material during the discussion.

Subjects will want to learn how to repeat this new listening experience by themselves. Most people feel they need two or three guided sessions before they can self-induce an ASC. In reality, the subjects are using self-induction even during the first guided session, for no guide can force anyone to enter an altered state without that individual's active cooperation. Whenever a subject reaches altered consciousness, he does so because he agrees to go along with the guide's suggestions. As soon as a person realizes that he can just as easily make similar suggestions to himself, he is ready for self-induction.

Some people have found it useful to make a tape or cassette recording of their own voice giving suggestions for relaxation and countdown. The recording then assumes the role of the guide.

Group Exercises

Any of the exercises for individuals presented in Chapter 3 may be adapted for group use.

It is important in group exercises to *keep suggestions short and simple.* Participants will generate more diversified and interesting responses if you leave details to individual imaginations. Simple suggestions allow for more personal structuring of the group experience.

Remember to include in each setting or exercise a final statement such as, "Let the music suggest where to go," or "Let the music take you wherever it wants you to go."

Inductions

Three additional relaxation and induction procedures have proven successful with a group: (1) energy inductions, (2) groaning and toning, and (3) movement procedures.

Energy Induction

The induction which follows was evolved from an idea developed by psychologist John Mann. It proposes relaxing people by putting them in touch with the universe, so that they begin to think of themselves as plugged into its power and energy sources. The group guide might use words such as these:

In a few minutes you will listen to some music, music that will take you to nonordinary places in your mind. Before you can enter this new level of consciousness, however, you must relax.

To do this, I suggest you lie down on your back.

Find a comfortable position. Remove anything like shoes or glasses that might keep you from being perfectly comfortable. Place your hands at your sides, or wherever they feel most at ease.

Once your body has found a relaxing position, perhaps moving about a bit to put everything in just the right place, you can begin to focus your attention on your breathing.

Think about your breath as it goes in and out. Watch it in your mind's eye. Enjoy the movement of your muscles as you inhale . . . and exhale. Continue to breathe normally, in and out. (Pause)

When you breathe in, your body takes in from the universe all that it needs. When you breathe out, you expel whatever your body does not need. You are giving back to the universe what you do not need, and receiving from it whatever you do need.

Enjoy visualizing your wonderful breathing system as it works to fill all of your body with nourishing oxygen. See the oxygen send energy through your lungs, into your heart, into your entire blood stream, carrying nourishment and energy outward into your arms and hands and fingers, down into your stomach and legs and feet, up into your shoulders and neck and face and brain.

Feel yourself as an integral part of the universe, as you breathe in and out, sharing willingly and comfortably with the universe everything you have and are. Enjoy being a part of the universe. (Pause)

Now imagine, outside of you, a ball in a tube. As you breathe in, the ball rises to the top of the tube. As you breathe out, the ball moves back downward.

Watch the ball for a few moments as it goes up and down in time with your breath. (Pause)

As your breath continues to keep time with the rise and fall of the ball, move the ball and tube inside your body. See it inside you, moving up and down just as before.

As you breathe in, the ball rises to the top of the tube; as you breathe out, it moves downward. With each breath you relax a little bit more. And, therefore, each time you breathe in, the ball rises less than the time before; each time you breathe out, it sinks a bit lower than before.

The ball will slowly sink lower and lower, and eventually come to settle in the pit of your stomach, just below your navel. This, we are told, is where the center of your being is located.

Take all the time you need, until the ball settles there. Let your breathing relax you. Watch the ball at it rises less and less, as it slowly sinks toward the center of your being, where it will come to rest, telling you that you are perfectly relaxed and that all your energies are now concentrated there . . . where the ball comes to rest . . . at the center of your being.

I will wait for a few moments while you watch the ball slowly come to rest in the center of your being. If it is there already, just enjoy your relaxation; deepen it until the ball is totally at rest. (Pause)

As the ball slowly comes to rest in the center of your being, you feel the focus of all your energies. We can test the energies located there. From the center of your being you can send energy to any part of your body.

Let's send some energy out to your fingertips. Begin slowly. Let the energy move out gradually from the center of your being. Send it upward toward your shoulder. Feel it, as it moves up through your stomach and chest. Let yourself experience the energy as it moves across your shoulder and begins the descent along your arm and into your hand.

Watch the energy work its way into your fingers. It is going to concentrate on one finger first, and make it tingle. Just to show its power, the energy will begin to make that finger tingle. Allow yourself to feel the tingling start.

Then the tingling will move to the next finger, then to the next, and the next, until all your fingers are tingling. Gradually the energy tingling will spread over the tops and bottoms of your fingers, then back across your hand, over the palm and across the back of your hand until your whole hand—up to your wrist—begins to tingle. Feel your energy telling you that it is there.

This is only a token of the vast energy at your disposal when you operate from the center of your being, as you are doing now.

Now that you are in touch with yourself, in control of the center of your being, in control of your sources of energy, enjoy it. Enjoy your relaxation. You are just about ready to enter a new level of consciousness.

Using your breath as a counter, follow a countdown from ten to zero. When you reach zero, you will be ready to let the music take you wherever it will.

With complete relaxation, then, and quiet anticipation, begin the countdown as you breathe. Ten . . . nine . . . more relaxed . . . eight . . . in touch with the center of your being . . . seven . . . six . . . more and more relaxed . . . five . . . coming toward your

*place . . . four . . . deeper and deeper into yourself
. . . three . . . still deeper . . . two . . . completely
relaxed . . . one . . . deeper and deeper . . . zero
. . . reaching your place, ready to let the music
take you wherever it will.*

At this point the musical program is begun.

At the conclusion of the music, the guide will help
the group return to ordinary consciousness with
words such as these:

*Now that we have had our experience, it is time
to return. Think of coming back to this room and
seeing once again the others here with you.*

*Think of the new experiences and insights you may
want to share with us. As you make your way back
to the room where we are gathered, I will count
from three to one. When I reach one you will open
your eyes, feeling relaxed and refreshed and ready
to share. Three . . . coming back now . . . two . . .
almost here . . . one . . . back in the room. Open
your eyes. Sit up and look around.*

A Ball of Energy

Here is another energy induction, based on a procedure used by John Lilly. It is described here in
slightly less detail than the previous one. In using
this induction, a guide may add additional suggestions and clarifications to suit particular listening
groups.

The induction presumes that the participants are
relaxed.

*Close your eyes and imagine a ball of energy in
your right hand. Let it begin as a small particle
and watch it grow into a huge ball. It is weightless,*

full of light, throbbing with energy from the universe.

Let the energy emanating from the huge ball slowly find a way to penetrate into your fingers and hand. Let it begin by passing through the pores of the skin. Because it is pure energy, it can do this easily.

Feel the energy now as it climbs up through your arm, filling with its power your bones, blood, muscles, and skin. Let your arm experience the new energy—energy you've never had before—coming to you from an inexhaustible source. The ball remains huge, bright, throbbing in your hand.

Watch the path of the energy as it moves across your shoulders and flows down the left side of your body, filling that whole side from shoulder to legs with new energy. Let the energy tingle in your skin; feel it tingle in your feet and toes. Let it get into every place inside you.

Now that your body begins to sense the new energy on this side, begin the process again, starting with a ball of energy in your left hand.

Watch it grow, then feel it go into your hands and up your arm, filling every part of you with new energy as it moves. Then feel it move across your shoulder and down the right side of your body, until it begins to make your right foot tingle.

By now your entire body is completely filled with new power and energy, which you can carry with you wherever you go.

Follow this procedure with a countdown into an altered state of consciousness. The best music to use here are selections filled with life, joy, enthusiasm—music that could make you want to get up and dance.

For the re-entry into normal consciousness, the guide can use the transition words suggested in the first energy induction.

Groaning and Toning

A very different technique for relaxation and induction of altered consciousness involves physical and vocal participation by group members. It is especially suitable for exercises involving intense emotions. The toning technique is adapted from Laurel Keyes, who describes it as an "expurgating process."

Lying comfortably on your back with your eyes closed, begin to groan. Let the groans be as deep and guttural as possible—the deeper the better— but without forcing. The groan is meant to release any form of tension, so the experience should be a pleasant, effortless one. Continue to groan.

You may feel a bit nervous or foolish about groaning in front of others, and you may giggle or laugh a bit. That's okay. Go ahead, let it out. Listen to the groaning all around you. It is a very releasing sound. You can almost visualize the group tension disappearing.

In order to make your groaning more satisfying, stretch your arms and legs as you would upon awakening. Then let your body relax, and groan again. You'll find it's deeper now, effortless and relaxing.

Let the groan come out from the depth of your being. You know how it feels when you have worked very hard, perhaps in tight clothing. Many women groan with relief when they remove their restrictive garments. Some people do it after taking off their tight shoes, while flexing their newly liberated feet and toes. Your groaning should be a comparable release. Let it be as loud as it comfortably can be.

Be sure to allow the groan to come from deep down. Too many people, especially those with tension, groan high up in their chests. The releasing groan comes from your heels. See how good it is.

As you learn to groan more freely, you'll notice a vibration starting in your body—maybe in the throat, perhaps in the chest, or maybe even in the stomach. Your body wants to vibrate throughout with that frequency; it wants to resonate with your groan. Let it.

As you continue to groan, you will feel a weight lifting from you, a psychic heaviness that is different from physical weight. As this heaviness is released, a sense of lightness grows within you. Simultaneously you will note a tendency of your voice to rise as all of your tensions or hurts are allowed to leave. If tears have been repressed, they are free to flow now. You are touching your body in a very deep way. Groaning is a healing process.

Let out whatever wants to come out. Whatever happens, you will begin to feel this natural desire in your voice to rise freely. Enjoy the feeling. Observe it. Allow it to happen. It is the body offering its best to something greater than itself. Just let your voice do what it wishes. It will find a natural resting place. Don't try to do, or not to do, anything. When your body reaches its tone, it will be satisfied, and you will sigh a deep satisfying sigh.

At this point you are toning: You are sounding your tone; feeling it as a perfect expression of you; feeling the vibrations of the tone in various places of your body—perhaps in your chest, your throat, *your nasal passages, or elsewhere.*

Enjoy your tone as part of the group tone. Don't try to create a specific harmony; just let the perfect sounds of your bodies blend together in their spontaneous harmony. This is your own music. Enter into it as a preparation for the other music we are to hear.

The guide may allow a few minutes for the toning to develop deeply. By that time, the group members should be well into altered states of consciousness. As they continue to tone, the guide may either begin the music directly (the group may automatically cease toning as it becomes conscious of the music), or he may present a visual setting followed by a ten-to-zero countdown as the group continues toning, beginning the music as he reaches zero.

At the close of the musical program, the guide simply suggests, as before, that the group members visualize themselves back in the listening room, feeling relaxed and refreshed; that they open their eyes at the count of three, finding themselves once again in ordinary consciousness.

The toning exercise may also be performed while standing: The group members stand near one another, eyes closed, feet about six inches apart. The lips should be barely open, to release the groan freely. In this erect posture, arm-stretching is particularly helpful. As in the prone toning, there is no conscious attempt to take deep breaths or to form particular words. However, people develop favorite toning sounds which they find most satisfying. A group that meets frequently might naturally develop some favorite group toning sounds. Many people use groaning and toning as a preparation for meditation, but it is also an excellent means to induce altered consciousness for music listening.

Movement Procedures

Many kinds of relaxing exercises and induction techniques involve muscular movements. A number of these have already been presented in other parts of this book. Muscle-relaxation exercises are universally effective in inducing a new consciousness. So, when first trying the new way to music with a group, a guide should begin with muscle-relaxing induction procedures.

Some readers may have learned muscle relaxing exercises elsewhere: In bio-energetics workshops, in Yoga classes, in natural childbirth training, in weight–watching programs or other activities that require a relaxed body. If such exercises are effective in bringing about relaxation for you, by all means use them. The basic rule is: Use whatever procedure best helps you to relax.

Exercise: Group Fantasy

Musical suggestions:
Bach, Concerto for Two Violins
Beethoven, Moonlight Sonata, *"Adagio"*
Beethoven, 6th Symphony (Pastoral)
Debussy, Nocturnes, *"Sirenes"*
Bill Evans, Peace Piece
French Music for the Harp
Hovhaness, Mysterious Mountain
Wagner, Siegfried's Rhine Journey

This exercise works well when introduced by the energy induction procedure given earlier in this chapter. The objective of the exercise is to generate an exprience that is shared by the entire group—a trip-in-common. During the relaxation and induction, the participants lie in a circle, their heads pointing toward its center (star formation), and holding hands.

The exercise is simply structured. When the music begins, one member spontaneously begins the fantasy by saying what he sees and how he feels. Keep the music volume low, so that people can easily hear each other. When the first member thinks he has described his fantasy sufficiently for others to enter it, he squeezes his neighbor's hand as a signal that the opportunity to develop fantasy is now transferred to him.

The new person carries the fantasy a step further, describing what he sees and how he feels, and then signals the next person, nonverbally inviting him to further unfold the original fantasy in similar images and symbols.

Allow enough time for the fantasy to unfold in detail. The symbols and images that recur again and again among the group during the program will provide matter for discussion and analysis after the exercise.

Either the guide or one of the participants may decide when the fantasy is complete. When that time arrives, the guide or selected participant suggests that all the members bring themselves back to the present and open their eyes after a one-two-three count.

Exercise: Group Grounding

This is a good exercise to build up waning group energy or to strengthen the group's sense of unity. Variations of the groaning and toning methods can be used by way of preparation.

The selection of music is important here: The strongest group feelings may be expected when peak experience music is played. (See appendix for suggested peak selections.) The guide, after the preparation, need only suggest that participants let the music take them wherever it will.

As the music begins, participants are asked to physically be "in touch with" something that *grounds them in reality*. The guide may suggest that holding onto another person is the most common psychological ground. However, some may want to begin the exercise alone. This is acceptable since not everyone will choose another person as ground. When grounded, an individual feels free to go into far-off spaces—to relinquish his hold on ordinary consciousness—yet feels assured that he is anchored to reality.

The guide's role in this exercise is to slowly bring people together. He should physically lead them toward one another, without a word, so that after a time—say twenty minutes or half an hour—all the participants are in the center of the room "tied together" by clasping hands. It is important, however, not to hurry people who are deeply into their personal experiences. The guide should return after a few minutes to ask them if they are now ready to join the group.

Exercise: Tribal Dance

One of the most valuable strengths of altered consciousness experience is its ability to generate large amounts of energy through group movement.

A movement technique or groaning and toning can be a suitable preparation for this exercise, since either kind of induction involves vigorous use of the body and prepares the participants physically for the tribal dance.

The music chosen should suggest a tribal dance—that is, it should be strongly rhythmic and emotional, and of sufficient duration and interest to allow for a variety of bodily movements and group responses. The *Missa Luba* is excellent music for the tribal dance. *Golden Rain,* an album of gamelan music (instrumental side), and any American Indian ceremonial music may also be used effectively. Much rock music may be appropriate. For a less vigorous experience, selections from the quiet listening suggestions listed in the appendix may be used.

The exercise is unstructured. As the music begins, the participants, who have been engaged in a physical movement induction, are asked simply to respond to the music in physical motion. They may move in pairs, in groups, or in isolation from one another. As the energy level increases, people become aware of their togetherness and shared strength.

Watusi jumping, an especially energizing technique, may be suggested. This is done by standing on slightly tipped toes and jumping as high as possible, continuously, until tired. Partners may do Watusi jumping facing each other, holding each other's shoulders, and jumping in unison.

After this experience, a group will be ready to brave anything together and to enjoy it.

Chapter 6

Music and Religious Experience

Religion has traditionally included music as an element in worship. Music can, however, contribute to other dimensions of the religious experience. That contribution can be even further enhanced when the music is experienced in a state of altered consciousness. This chapter explores some new frontiers of religion and music.

Our tradition teaches us that sound is God—Nada Brahma. That is, musical sound and the musical experience are steps to the realization of the self. We view music as a kind of spiritual discipline that raises one's inner being to divine peacefulness and bliss. We are taught that one of the fundamental goals a Hindu works toward in his lifetime is a knowledge of the true meaning of the universe—its unchanging, eternal essence—and this is realized first by a complete knowledge of one's self and one's own nature. The highest aim of our music is to reveal the essence of the universe it reflects, and the ragas are among the means by which this essence can be apprehended. Thus, through music, one can reach God.

Ravi Shankar

Sunday, After a Wedding

After a recent wedding, several friends stayed overnight at the same home. Next morning, Sunday, the weather was damp and stormy, and no one was eager to dress up in Sunday best and brave the snow and slush to church.

Instead, a religious experience at home in the living room was suggested, and the idea of listening to music in altered states of consciousness was explained. Some were more curious than others, but all were willing to try a group experience. Seven people, aged seventeen to forty, were asked to lie down comfortably on the floor or on a couch, close their eyes, and follow the suggestions.

When they were sufficiently relaxed, the session began with the second movement of Beethoven's *Pastoral Symphony*, and continued with appropriate musical selections for the next forty-five minutes. Afterwards, they were asked to sit up and share with each other what they had experienced. Most of them were surprised to find they had entered new mind-spaces during the music—spaces they had never known existed. Each one affirmed that he had had what he considered a religious experience.

Music and Religious Meditation

A short time ago, a religious sister completing her doctoral research work in clinical psychology was introduced to the consciousness-altering technique. Her interest in a new way to music focused on the possibilities of new kinds of religious experience.

In fact, it sometimes happens that the whole tone and atmosphere of a person's life of prayer—a certain emphasis on solitude or on sacrifice or on apostolic radiation—is provided by elements in the subconscious mind. For the subconscious mind is a storehouse of images and symbols, I might almost say of "experiences" which provides us with more than half the material of what we actually experience as "life." Without our knowing it, we see reality through glasses colored by the subconscious memory of previous experiences.

Thomas Merton

During a weekend workshop for sisters on values clarification, she introduced music listening in altered states as an alternate way into prayer and meditation.

Gathered together were about twenty sisters, none older than thirty, who had come to their motherhouse-novitiate for a month of prayer and conferences preparatory to taking their final vows. Since they had arrived that very day from their various schools, hospitals, and residences, they were reestablishing acquaintances, slowly beginning to feel at home with each other. There was some tension in the group, and concern about families, schools, and homes—for the weekend began at the height of flood disasters from a hurricane. It was also the end of a hectic school year and most of the sisters were exhausted when the first listening experience took place Friday night.

One sister, who was very tired and, therefore, did not have her usual control over herself, subsequently described her reactions as "surprised and frightened." It was difficult for her to discuss her very intense experiences which had included feeling herself as outside her body.

It is the religious question which is asked when the poet opens up the horror and fascination of the demonic regions of his soul, or if he leads us into the deserts and empty places of our being, or if he shows the physical and moral mud under the surface of life, or if he sings the song of transitoriness, giving words to the ever-present anxiety of our hearts.

Paul Tillich

Although fear and disturbance often indicate the presence of personal psychological problems, this sister's disturbance was more due to the surprise and apprehension of a new, mind-expanding adventure. Her experiences had, in fact, been very profound and mystical.

"I found myself a part of God," she said later, "totally existing in him and responding with him to the approaches of others, until everyone else was consumed by my God and we shared the same vision."

For most people, religion has always been a matter of traditional symbols and of their own emotional, intellectual and ethical response to those symbols. To men and women who have had direct experience of self-transcendence into the mind's Other World of vision and union with the nature of things, a religion of mere symbols is not likely to be very satisfying. The perusal of a page from even the most beautifully written cookbook is no substitute for the eating of dinner. We are exhorted to "taste and see that the Lord is good."

Aldous Huxley

Two listening sessions were offered; attendance was optional. Before each session, a different relaxation–induction procedure was followed. The method of tensing and relaxing individual muscles from toe to head seemed most effective.

One sister had previously tried music as an aid for meditation. She came to the sessions "to see what I could learn about myself from the music."

Like many others, she was surprised at the depth of consciousness she could plumb. In a report on her second session, she described going out of her body at the outset, accompanied by images of lightness and motion. "I was dancing a ballet."

There still remain to us techniques of training the mind-body to a more normal way of life in which faith is not a conscientious effort of the mind to believe, but a normal functioning of spirit that pervades and animates and gives wholeness to an instrument in which no part can work alone.

Jennette Lee

Later the guide gave the group an additional countdown to reach greater depths of consciousness. "I was eager to see what would come, how much deeper I could go into myself." During the next musical selection she reported she felt very much part of a religious procession.

Lots of pageantry at first, fine clothes, orchestra, a crowd of people, happy faces. Then candles, a simple atmosphere, but still religious—a kind of me-and-God relationship. More joy, a sense of power, and shared joy of a large group. My personal ability and power.

When she sat up to share her experiences, she felt "a kind of heaviness, a very slow return to the present, a not wanting to come back, a sudden awareness of my body." She found it much more difficult to discuss her experiences than at the previous session. "This experience was much deeper," she explained. "It helped me to realize what control I have over my body, and how well-chosen musical selections can help me find my space and, on other occasions, different spaces."

I have been concerned with the creation of music for more than thirty years, with no lessening of my sense of humility before the majesty of music's expressive power, before its capacity to make manifest a deeply spiritual resource of mankind.

Aaron Copland

Confusion and bewilderment at coming back to normal consciousness seemed to be a frequent reaction among this group of young sisters. One was able to isolate her problem. "So many of my fears at this point are tied up with finding myself and where I am going . . . During the experience the music became a part of me and expressed what I am, and where I am, at this point." But she was not "ready to say it to anyone. I found it difficult to discuss my experiences because they disclose my own fears about myself."

An Anonymous Sister

Others had deeply religious experiences which they hesitated to share. One sister mailed them to the workshop director anonymously. During the afternoon listening session, her mood had been one of great excitement:

A yellow, yellow-orange universe. Colors seemed to coalesce, merge into a swirling ball which turned into a ferris wheel! (I've hated ferris wheels —or probably should say I've always been afraid of them, and I don't think I've ever ridden one.) I was awed, then sort of delighted that this turned into a ferris wheel. But then, while everyone was on the ferris wheel, it changed into a large white [communion] host!

After being on the ferris-wheel/host and then dismembering myself from it, I went to God, who was playing ball!!! A bouncing ball—and he was bouncing along with it—a sort of slow-motion-photography kind of bounce.

Then all of us merged into a terrific ballet/praise, and he smiled and the universe was all soft yellow-orange again.

Her next experience she found the most rewarding.

I was caught up in the universe, the offering of the universe, and of all being. This probably pre-conditioned my Sunday afternoon image of finding God. It had to be God—so alive, shiny, and open to us, but so simple, even playful, relating to a group of four people (I was one of them) with effortless sincerity. And he was [Pierre de] Chardin —at least he looked just like photos I've seen of Chardin. This was completely satisfactory to me ... Seeing God like this was so easy to respond to, to interact with!

I was anxious to see if this satisfied feeling would

last. It has till now, Tuesday. But will it be there in November when school and convent get hectic?

Results of the Sisters' Weekend

Although listening to music was only a secondary part of the values weekend, the new music experience drew the sisters' strongest response and interest. For many, the listening experiences proved to be a significant milestone in personal growth; for some it was self-revelatory; for others, a generally liberating experience.

As a result of the weekend, some felt that music in nonordinary consciousness offered a new way to prayer. Others, who had been having difficulty praying in the recent past, felt that this could be a way to help them pray well again.

One sister, who had found the traditional forms of prayer restrictive, summarized her listening sessions "as an experience in which I can let myself be free." Her attitude toward prayerful experiences in general also changed radically.

There is a spiritual, or religious, or even metaphysical hunger among young people which standard brand religions just don't satisfy. For one thing, the standard brand religions have had a cardinal defect for centuries now. They preach. They tell you what you ought to do, but they are not sources of power. In other words, they do not transform the way you feel, the way you experience your own existence or your own identity. They just talk and urge.

Alan Watts

"I felt I was being impelled to determine and examine my values," said another sister. Still another spoke of experiences in altered consciousness as "adding a new dimension to my life."

Although there were a few who found the music experiences unsatisfying, most of the sisters were eager to further explore the possibilities of prayer and worship in altered states of consciousness with music.

Perhaps the briefest way to indicate the nature of this atmosphere is to quote a remark that is frequently made at these group workshops, namely, "This is what I would like to have happen in church, but it almost never does."

Ira Progoff

At the Transpersonal Psychology Meetings

Extraordinarily exciting experiences with music happened in 1972 at the Iceland meeting of the First International Conference on Psychobiology and Transpersonal Psychology. For one week, over sixty people, aged nineteen to ninety, from all over the world, took over Bifrost, a fashionable summer resort in the lava field wilderness of Iceland, at the foot of a majestic volcanic crater. Surrounded by the unspoiled beauty of arctic nature in the land of the midnight sun, psychologists, anthropologists, mythologists, artists, scientists, historians, psychiatrists, healers, theologians, and many others gathered to share their pathways to transpersonal experience.

**The general trend of development in science espe-
cially in recent decades seems to indicate that the
scientific concepts of the future will increasingly ap-
proximate those of the mystical and religious systems. Thus, for example, modern concepts of time,
space, energy and matter are approaching those of
the Vedic philosophy and religion. The same can be
said about the discoveries in contemporary psychology and psychiatry; Jung's analytical psychology,
Assagioli's psychosynthesis, Abraham Maslow's concept of man, as well as the results of the exploration
of the human mind with the use of psychedelic sub-
stances are easily compatible with many ancient mystical and religious systems.**

Stanislav Grof

The purpose of the conference was to bring together scientific researchers from disciplines related
to the study of consciousness, to exchange and integrate information, to discuss specific methodologies
and formulate new directions for research efforts.
Special emphasis was placed on altered states of consciousness, psychobiology, transcendental states and
psychic healing.

No formal papers were read. Rather, long periods
of time were available for participants to work together. Thus, in an afternoon it was possible to cross
paths with experts in voluntary control of internal
states, meditation, psychedelic drugs, hypnosis,
dreams, autogenic training, sensory isolation, mysti-
cism, psychic healing, spiritual healing, transpersonal
growth, and brain biochemistry.

Geir Vilhjalmsson, director of the Institute for Consciousness Research, in Reykjavik, Iceland, was one of the conference's originators. His Institute sponsored the conference, together with the Transpersonal Association of Palo Alto, California.

Two music listening sessions were offered to the entire group. For many it was the first transpersonal experience with music.

The Truth Diamond

In spring the Icelandic sun doesn't set until midnight, so the first musical session was held in the large conference room at 9 p.m. The session began with a groaning and toning exercise and a meditation led by Geir. Then they were helped to relax, and the following program was played:

Beethoven's Piano Concerto #5, (Emperor), *2nd movement*
Elgar's Enigma Variations, *#9*
Mozart's Laudate Dominum
Gounod's St. Cecilia Mass, *"Sanctus"*
Strauss' Death and Transfiguration, *"Transfiguration"*

The meditation which Geir developed was based on the ancient diamond path of Tibetan Buddhism. The deep roots of the diamond symbol are well illustrated by the following myth developed by one of the participants in response to the meditation.

In ancient times there lived a people in a beautiful country, working the land, enjoying loving relationships. The leaders of the people felt they had earned the right to receive the Truth.

About that time, a shining prophet appeared among them. He was greatly revered, for they believed he possessed the Truth.

One day, the prophet led all the people to the foot

*of a mountain. He himself climbed to the top, hold-
ing the huge Truth diamond above his head. The
people fell to their knees, smitten by the blinding
light reflected through the diamond.*

*Then, with all his force, the prophet dashed the
giant diamond to the ground, breaking it into millions of tiny pieces. Then he disappeared, as mys-
teriously as he had come.*

*People scavenged for days collecting pieces of the
diamond, which they called pieces of Truth. Pieces
of the Truth diamond became family treasures.
Jealousy and envy grew, as people built walls
around their diamond pieces.*

*Each had a fragment of Truth, but not the whole
Truth; and none was willing to give up his fragment. This was the origin of strife in the world.*

At the end of the meditation, Geir suggested that
everyone in the group begin to visualize a diamond
growing above his or her head, with each individual
diamond rising above the group to form one huge
diamond. At this point, the musical program began.

Winifred Laurance, involved for many years in
transpersonal experience, described her response to
the diamond meditation:

*As Geir led us in consciousness higher and higher
into light, and then to the visualization of the diamond above his head, I felt an increasing sense of
excitement and anticipation. Then, as each individual diamond was set high above to join with
all the others to form one very large diamond, I
was filled with an overwhelming sensation of ex-
ultation and joy, so vast as to be almost cosmic in
scope. This emotion, deep within the planet as well*

as within me, might be put into words as, "We have waited so long for this." I watched as the rays of the sun pierced the great prisms of the many-faceted diamond, and hundreds of rainbows began to sparkle from it.

At this point the music began and as the orchestral chorale swelled further with deep organ-like tones, four angels—great shining entities—appeared from the north, south, east and west, each taking a point of the diamond. They carried it swiftly to a place in the sky directly above the North Pole.

Almost at once I was aware of individual diamonds and larger group diamonds ascending from all parts of the earth and becoming a part of our great diamond which grew even larger and larger. The sun continued to send its rays, now creating thousands of rainbows. The rainbows joined themselves end to end, and formed great bridges of color and light joining the North and South Poles, marking off sections like the longitudinal lines on a globe. As the piano music began with sparkling cascades of notes, bright crystal drops, more like dew drops than jewels, rolled from the great diamond and cascaded over the rainbow bridge to the South Pole and then spread out from the bridge as latitudinal lines around the earth.

I looked upon the earth from outer space and saw it encased in a shimmering network of color and light. Then I seemed to identify myself with the earth itself, and as I looked up into the rainbow the living water droplets began to shower down refreshment and purity.

As the piano concert ended and the next selection —I think it was strings and woodwinds—I became identified first with nature and felt its response to

*our love and desire to heal. The animals, birds, in-
sects, plants, and even the mountains, rocks, and
soil reacted. With the prelude to the soprano solo
my thoughts turned to humanity, and great waves
of gratitude and love washed over me—gratitude
and love both for humanity and from humanity.*

*The music of the tenor solo brought joy and ap-
preciation of the Christ. The Sanctus was the com-
bined response of the nature kingdom and humanity to Christ, and the finale included the recognition by other planets of our solar system, that at
long last the earth is beginning to shine with its
own light.*

**Music in all ages has given man a sense of mystical
but immediate kinship with the transcendent and the
universal.**

J. H. Masserman

Another participant, Dr. Arthur Joseph Brodbeck,
director of the Human Potentials Institute in New
York, transformed the mythical diamonds into a
cluster of stars, and found himself among these stars,
penetrating deeper and deeper into the universe.

At this point a child walked into the room where
the participants were listening. Dr. Brodbeck was dis-
tracted by the child's presence, but watched her in
joy until she left.

*After that, I went back into a deep meditation
where there was no imagery, just a quiet, warm,
joyful feeling. I had a feeling of being pulled out
of my body. The rest of the time was associated
with an out-of-the-body experience. I didn't really*

hear the musical selections, nothing at all jarred
my state.

During the last piece, I came back to my body
slowly and gently. I emerged from the experience
peacefully, with feelings of warmth and joy which
lasted through most of the evening.

A Peak Experience

A psychotherapist from Baltimore also attended
the conference. During the first listening session,
lying beside his wife, he had a peak experience of
high intensity. This is his report:

I lay on my back, flat on the floor, and smoothly
slid into a state of profound muscular relaxation.
My legs and arms felt heavy and detached; it
seemed that the only way they could be moved
would be through a conscious decision and com-
mand, followed by considerable effort. I heard
Helen's voice leading the group in relaxation exercises, suggesting that certain muscles be tightly
contracted and then allowed to relax but, in spite
of a few feeble attempts, I was unable (and unwilling) to contract any muscles in my body. It
seemed as though my motor nervous system had
been turned off, and there seemed no point in
reactivating it.

Eventually, I heard the opening strains of the
slow movement of Beethoven's Emperor Concerto,
welcomed them, and experienced an aesthetically
pleasing sense of flowing with the music. Caught
up in its relentless, yet gentle, motion, I was
carried higher and higher towards some ethereal,
pure white mountain top, bathed in golden sunlight.

During Mozart's "Laudate Dominum" I found myself moving towards more profoundly meaningful
experiences. I recognized that I was entering mystical dimensions of consciousness that previously
I had known only with the assistance of psychedelic drugs. The inner space continued to expand and become increasingly filled with light.
The sense of movement continued towards the
beautiful form of a goddess, reminiscent of the
Virgin Mary; then, it seemed as though I passed
through this form and, in so doing, shifted to another level of consciousness.

From this point on, it becomes very difficult to
describe the experience. My ego, or usual sense of
self, would re-emerge, usually at the beginning of
a new section of the music. I recognized Elgar's
Ninth Variation, the "Sanctus" from Gounod's
Saint Cecilia Mass and the "Transfiguration" section from Richard Strauss' Death and Transfiguration. Then, however, it would cease to "observe"
or "exist" and would dissolve into a realm of
eternal essence. There seemed to be movement
back and forth between essence and existence,
between transcendent forms of consciousness and
my usual state of being. My dominant feelings
were those of love and tenderness, and, most of
all, of joy. As the ecstasy grew in intensity, I
found tears running down my cheeks. Intuitively,
I realized that all human suffering was compas-
sionately integrated into the vast, exquisitely beautiful, multidimensional structure of ultimate, unitive Being. Clearly, from this perspective, there
could be no basis for anxiety. Time did not exist—
only an eternal awareness that encompassed the
past and the future. There was no death, only

transmutation of energy from one form to another, and perhaps to yet another and another.

In a flash, I thought of an elderly Negro patient to whom I had said goodbye on leaving for Iceland. We both knew that he would be dead before I returned. Now I seemed to be on the boundary of the eternal world, welcoming him with open arms and saying, with a certain bemusement, "See, I didn't abandon you at all."

I sensed that my wife, who was lying on the floor beside me, was also deeply involved in similar experience. At times I wanted to touch her to express some form of physical communication, but the effort was simply too great. Finally, I touched her side lightly with the tips of my fingers. In response, she took my hand and placed it on her abdomen and on the child she was carrying within herself. At that point, my joy became so intense as to be almost unbearable and tears flowed down my face. The miracle of our child's reality was incredibly wonderful. I believed that I emitted some sobbing sounds at that time as expressions of ecstasy. I perceived footsteps around my head and realized that not all the participants were as deeply involved in their experiences as I was; yet, the presence of other people did not inhibit the experiences within my own psyche.

Reports from the Icelandic sessions show the broad range of experiences that fall under the heading of religious or transpersonal experience. Some of the cases presented here involve high level transcendent experiences; others are less significant. Prayer in altered states of consciousness is an area that calls for much exploration.

Chapter 7

Exercises for Religious Experience

Consciousness and Religious Experience

It is clear from the previous chapter, that the term religious experience is not used here in any restrictive sense. Rather, it designates a continuum of transpersonal experiences, allowing each reader to bring to the listening experience his own ideas about man, nature, God, religion, and the transcendent.

The human consciousness contains many transpersonal spaces. Such interrelated terms as prayer, meditation, contemplation, spiritual conversion experiences, speaking in tongues, unitive experience, living in God, acting in the Spirit, refer to these mental realms and traditionally are often called "religious experience."

Peak experience is sometimes confused with religious experience, but the two concepts are separable: A religious experience can be a peak, but it need not be. Similarly, one may have a peak experience which is not primarily religious.

It is important here to make two qualifications: The first is that none of the following exercises can guarantee a religious or transcendent experience. They have proved helpful in bringing certain individuals to various transpersonal spaces; hopefully they will prove equally helpful to many readers.

The second qualification is to note that religious experience can happen at any time, unpredictably. It is quite possible, for instance, for someone engaged in one of the individual or group exercises to be carried by the music into a transpersonal space. This is more likely to happen to those with a particularly religious orientation.

Exercise: Opening of the Senses

Musical suggestions:

Bach, Mass in B Minor, "Gloria"
Britton, A Ceremony of Carols
Holst, The Planets, "Venus"
Rachmaninoff, Symphony #2, Adagio

After relaxation and induction procedures, suggest that the music take you to a place where there are various textures and surfaces to touch and feel.

When you arrive, slowly explore your surroundings. Let the music help you experience softness and smoothness. Feel the contours and texture of things. Let each object express itself to you. Hold it in your hand, let it touch your face, your nose, your tongue, other parts of your skin. There is no need to rush from one touch to another; take time to savor each tactile sensation.

Then let each surface or object take you back to its source. Discover where it comes from, why it feels as it does, how it comes to be here, now. The deeper you can go into the origin and meaning of the experience, the richer the transpersonal experience will be.

Note: This exercise can also be performed using sense modalities other than touch; namely sight, hearing, smell, taste, and other kinesthetic senses related to temperature, pain, and so on.

Exercise: My Flower

Musical suggestions:
Debussy, Girl with the Flaxen Hair
Tchaikovsky, "A Golden Cloudlet" (see Oberlin Choir in Russia)
Tchaikovsky, The Nutcracker Suite, *"Waltz of the Flowers"*

As the music begins, let it take you on a search for a special flower, one that is to be your unique flower in the world. You may come to a beautiful garden, go walking along a mountain path, or find yourself near a hidden lake. Wherever the music takes you, you will find your flower. There may be many flowers to choose from, but one flower will stand out: You will recognize it as soon as you see it.

Once you find it, there will be only you and your flower. You will be able to communicate with it, and in time it will reveal itself to you, including the many levels of meaning it holds for your life. Try to formulate for your flower the questions with deepest significance for you.

In answering, the flower may take you to different places, as if it were your guide. Follow it wherever it goes. Remember, its reason for being is to help you answer any questions you may have.

Exercise: The Love Collector

Musical suggestions:

Brahms, Violin Concerto, *2nd movement*
Holst, The Planets, *"Venus"*
Mantovani, Songs to Remember, Sentimental Strings

Let the music take you anywhere it wishes. You will find there some person or object that you like very much, or that likes you very much. If you can't immediately find something you like very much, you will certainly be able to find something you can learn to like, or someone who is learning to like you. Start with that.

Bring the object of your affection so close that you feel the love vibrations moving between the two of you. Then begin looking for a second person or object you like, and again bring it close to you. Repeat this procedure many times until you find no one or nothing else that fits the qualifications. Before you stop collecting, however, be completely sure that you have exhausted your supply of likeables and loveables.

As your collection comes to you, ask each person or object why you like them or why they like you, how this love came about and how it can be fostered, now and in the future. Surrounded by your love collection, allow the vibrations among you to grow and grow. You have brought all these together to let them know that they are liked and loved by you. In return, let them express their love for you.

As the music comes to a close, send each of your loves back to its original place. You will return to ordinary consciousness knowing that everywhere in the universe you are accepted and loved.

Exercise: Loving a Nobody

Musical suggestions:

Barber, Adagio for Strings
Bernstein, Chichester Psalms III, "Psalm 131"
Brahms, The German Requiem, *Part I*
Canteloube, Songs of the Auvergne
Rachmaninoff, Vocalise
Villa-Lobos, Bachianas Brasileras, #5

Let the music take you to a place where you will find a nobody—a person about whom no one seems to care. The nobody may be hard to find at first because he will be in a place where no one would ever think to look.

Once you find him (or her), discover all you can without disturbing him. Examine the surroundings, the smells, the light, the darkness, the noise, the silence. Then look closely at him. You can approach as closely as you wish, for you are invisible to him. You will be able to look into his eyes, feel his pulse, read the lines in his face. Each of his features will tell you something about him.

As the music helps you reach into his feelings, his wishes, his needs, it will allow him to communicate unconsciously with you. Let his history unfold before you—the events of his life, the feelings that accompanied them. Then let him tell you, still unconsciously, how he came to be a nobody, and what he might have been and might yet be if . . .

The music will invite you to respond to his need, to his longing. Allow feelings of concern and compassion (not pity and sorrow) to well up within you and flow out to him. Let their strength increase, until you can see him stir in response.

If you feel that your love energy will not be powerful enough to transform the nobody, call upon the energy of the universe. Let it flow through you into him, until he is reborn, until he begins to realize that he is not a nobody, but a person who has at his disposal all the powers of the universe.

As the music comes to a close, reflect on your own feelings at being a part of this event in a nobody's life.

Exercise: The Truth Diamond

Musical suggestions:

Beethoven, Piano Concerto #5 (Emperor), *Adagio*
Elgar, Enigma Variations, #8, 9
Gounod, St. Cecilia Mass, *"Offertory," "Sanctus," "Bene-
dictus"*
Mozart, "Laudate Dominum," "Vesperas"
Strauss, Death and Transfiguration, *"Transfiguration"* (only)

The Tibetan parable of the truth diamond presented in the previous chapter may be used as a
meditative setting preceding a listening experience.
The musical portion of the exercise remains totally
unstructured. Simply let the music suggest whatever
it will.

If this exercise is done in a group, a discussion
and sharing session should follow.

Any symbolic story, myth, parable, or event may
be used in this way, beginning with the narrative,
then moving into the music. Biblical stories, religious
parables, traditional prayers, even certain fairy tales
may be quite effective as preparatory meditative material.

Exercise: A Love Supreme

Musical suggestion:

John Coltrane, A Love Supreme, *"Psalm"*

The album jacket of *A Love Supreme* by John
Coltrane, jazz tenor sax soloist, carries a psalm
written by Coltrane. This text may be read reflec-
tively before the music begins, or while it plays.
Many people have found it deeply satisfying to have
someone slowly read the psalm aloud to a group
listening in altered consciousness.

For those who cannot find *A Love Supreme*, an-

other recording by Coltrane or albums by other re-
flective jazz artists—Miles Davis, Thelonius Monk,
Paul Horn, to mention only a few—may be used in
a similar way with appropriate readings, such as
biblical psalms, hymn lyrics, or religious poetry.

Exercise: Hymns and Spiritual Songs

Musical suggestions:

Ernest Bloch: Sacred Service
Tennessee Ernie Ford, Hymns
Mahalia Jackson, Abide With Me, Let's Pray Together
N. Luboff Choir, Inspiration
Johnny Mathis, Good Night, Dear Lord
Mormon Tabernacle Choir, The Beloved Choruses, I, II
The Robert Shaw Chorale, Deep River

Following a relaxation and induction procedure, a
program of hymns or choir music may be reverently
listened to in altered states of consciousness, allowing the music to take you wherever it will.

This exercise may be used as a period of thanks-
giving or praise following prayers or spiritual reading, alone with one's family or in a group. It may be
used following a church service, to generate deeper
sharing among a group.

Exercise: Gratitude

Musical suggestions:
Bach, "Jesus, Dearest Master"
Bach, St. Matthew Passion, Aria: "Erbarmedich, Mein Gott"
Kirsten Flagstad, Wagner and Brahms Songs
Misa Criolla (folk mass)
Palestrina, Stabat Mater

Allow the music to take you successively to a
series of places or situations where the forces of life

and growth are most obviously at work. Enter as deeply as you can into these living elements, see them as a gift of a loving source of all life. Formulate some word or gesture of gratitude specifically for each element.

This exercise may be done in the group, allowing various forms of grateful expression. Leave the medium of expression open, or suggest to the participants that their acts of gratitude be expressed nonverbally. In this latter context, creativity is developed and enhanced.

Exercise: At-one-ment

Musical suggestions:

Bach, B Minor Mass, "Credo"
Brahms, The German Requiem, Parts 4, 5, and 7
Faure, Requiem, "Sanctus," "In Paradisium," "Pie Jesu"
Gounod, St. Cecilia Mass
Tschesnekoff, "Salvation is Created"
Vivaldi, Gloria, "Et in Terra Pax"

One's fellowship with all humanity and unity with the totality of nature may be explored while listening to the musical selections listed here.

Let the music take you where it wants to. Wherever you go, you will be able to find at least two objects which are interdependent and interconnected in nature. Focus your attention on the bond between them. Find a third object, see how it can be linked with the first two, then a fourth, a fifth, and so on, until you can interconnect whatever object appears into a single whole.

Establishing unity among human beings normally takes the form of reconciliation or at-one-ment. As people begin to appear during your experience, try to find a way to bring them together in human unity, without conflict or competition. Let the procedure continue until you have discovered the bonds holding everyone and everything together, and until the feeling of oneness you have helped bring about erupts spontaneously from the group in song, shout, dance, or other forms of expression.

Allow yourself to feel at one with them, and join in their response.

Exercise: Cosmic Vibrations

Musical suggestions:

Monks of Solemes, Gregorian Chants
Alan Hovhaness, Fra Angelico
Paul Horn, Inside
R. Strauss, Thus Spake Zarathustra

Some scientists tell us that there is no void in the universe, that what appears as empty space is really filled to overflowing with many kinds of waves: cosmic rays, x-rays, radio waves, light waves, television signals, auditory waves, and many others. They tell us that colors, too, are simply visible waves; that the atmosphere and even matter itself are huge concentrations of vibrating waves, each with its own frequency or pulse.

When the music begins, allow it to take you to a place where you can begin to understand the universe as one vast vibrating cosmos. You may begin the experience on a small scale, seeing one element as part of the cosmic vibration, then another, then a third, and so on, until you are able to grasp the vibrating fullness of the universe and integrate yourself with it.

Let the music show you the meaning behind these cosmic vibrations.

Chapter 8

Music Appreciation in the Classroom

The Goals of Music Appreciation

One of the most potent settings for experiment and training in the new way to music is the classroom, since nowadays students from kindergarten to college attend music appreciation classes.

The child grows in a world of sound and comes to school with a relatively complex sense for its use. He can distinguish different meanings in slight alterations of soft sounds. He knows serenity in the sounds of ocean waves and lullabies, the expectancy of hushed voices, the terror of whispers in the night. He understands joys, power, and fear in the varied timbres of loud sounds and can even focus his attention on a single meaningful sound—say the jingle of the ice-cream truck—above the din. The child has developed a kind of musicality, for what else is music made of, but sounds with meaning, sounds which stir the sense of expectancy, of climax, of repose?

Barbara Hurley

Listening with a heightened consciousness would not in any way negate or minimize the present goals of music appreciation. It would enhance and support them. The new way to music offers a more intensified approach to listening, a technique of appreciation that can be learned by students in a short time and at no additional expense.

Appreciation requires attentive listening. The approach suggested in this book uses a technique for achieving heightened awareness, which has not been taught in classrooms before.

It's not easy to listen to a piece and really know and feel what's going on in it all the time. It may be easy to take, **or pleasant to hear for many people; it may evoke fanciful images in the mind, or bathe them in a sensuous glow, or stimulate, or soothe, or whatever. But none of that is** listening. **And until we have a great listening public, and not just a passively** hearing **one, we will never be a musically cultured nation.**

Leonard Bernstein

Through exercises in relaxation and concentration, students are shown how to reach an altered state of consciousness which enables them to experience musical selections with heightened awareness and a fresh sense of reality.

Teachers of music appreciation routinely use programmed music to provide interest and stimulation for students. A bee is the subject of Rimsky-Korsakov's "Flight of the Bumblebee"; thunder and wind are depicted in "Cloudburst" from Grofe's *Grand Canyon Suite;* "Morning" by Grieg describes the sunrise. Experienced in altered states of consciousness, such selections can help individual students in their imaginative forays, and their experiences can then be shared in discussion with the whole class.

Imagination is a function which in itself is to some extent synthetic, since imagination can operate at several levels concurrently: those of sensation, feeling, thinking and intuition . . . The imagination, in the precise sense of the function of evoking and creating images, is one of the most important and spontaneously active functions of the human psyche, both in its conscious and in its unconscious aspects or levels.

Roberto Assagioli

Symphonies, operas, concertos, sonatas, dances, marches, hymns, chorales, vocal music, folk songs, popular music, jazz, electronic music—every kind of music can be enjoyed and experienced more fully by listening in the new way.

Though it might seem that the new way to music would be more effective with programmatic music than with music devoid of descriptive content, this is not necessarily true. The nondescriptive element of pure music can offer the listener an open-ended setting for creative spontaneous experience.

Some Answers to Questions Teachers Ask

What type of music is best for music appreciation classes?

There are no limitations on music genre, although programmatic music seems best for beginners.

Use selections that maintain a constant mood. People need time to enter into a newly suggested emotion. Hence, pieces with abruptly changing emotional moods are not suitable for initial satisfactory listening experience in altered consciousness.

It is important to avoid music whose mood is in any way negative, threatening or frightening. Since experiences are magnified and intensified in a state of altered consciousness, such music may upset the listener.

How long should a musical selection last?

For younger children, a listening program should last from five to ten minutes. Older students can profit from longer programs, depending on the length of the class period.

Be sure to allow enough time before the selection for relaxation and induction, after the selection for transition back to normal consciousness, and for discussion so that every listener has a chance to share his experience with the group if he so wishes.

What about the technical quality of the record or tape used in a listening session?

Ideally, the recordings used should be free of cracks or other annoying surface noise, for sound experiences are magnified in an altered state of consciousness. The best reproduction of music tends to generate the fullest experience in the listeners, because in hi-fidelity reproduction there is *simply more to be heard.*

Through music a child enters a world of beauty, expresses his inmost self, tastes the joy of creating, widens his sympathies, develops his mind, soothes and refines his spirit and adds grace to his body.

                              The United States National
                              Child Welfare Association

What are the usual student fears before experience

of altered consciousness?

That the whole idea is silly; that it will never work; that they won't experience anything. A few students fear that they might lose control; that they will reveal embarrassing things about themselves; that others will disapprove of what they do or say.

What are the typical questions students ask about the altered consciousness experience?

In general, students ask the same questions that everyone else asks: How will it feel? How do I know I'm in altered consciousness? What if I don't go into an altered state? How does it happen, psychologically? Could I ever get stuck in this state? How much control over myself will I have while there? These questions are fully answered elsewhere in this book.

What is the teacher's best preparation for a classroom listening session in altered states of consciousness?

Try out on yourself exactly what you plan to do during class. Listen in altered consciousness to the musical selection(s) you have chosen. This experience will provide material to initiate the class discussion, and also guarantee that the musical selection is appropriate for altered consciousness.

When selecting recordings to play, remember that with heightened consciousness everything is intensified and magnified—positive and negative experiences alike. For example, if during a selection characterized by joy there are a few measures of sad or somber music, the listener in altered consciousness can experience a strong mood change at that point, while the normal listener would not be affected at all. For this reason, teachers are advised to try on themselves each program they plan to use with their students.

What can teachers do who are assigned to teach a certain "list" of musical selections?

For most of the selections on an assigned list, as well as for favorite pieces that are not presented in this book, teachers can creatively develop settings and inductions for listening in altered states of consciousness.

When preparing an induction, listen to the selection first, then classify it according to mood. This will help you design an induction and setting that matches the mood of the music.

How does a guide go about developing inductions for use in the classroom?

A number of sample inductions for use with groups of various age-levels are given elsewhere in the book. Once teachers recognize the steps of an induction, they may create their own inductions or adapt sample inductions to their own needs.

Is it best to always use the same induction technique?

A familiar and previously successful induction usually succeeds in helping induce altered consciousness. However, once a particular technique is established, students welcome a variety of inductions.

After several exercises have been carried out successfully with a classroom group, induction and countdown may be minimized or dropped, since by this time students will be able to go easily into the music. Usually, it will suffice simply to say to them, "Relax in the best way for you, and go with the music."

You will find a number of sample inductions and exercises specifically designed for classroom use in the following pages.

Chapter 9

Exercises for the Classroom

Practical Hints for Classroom Exercises

The tone of voice is one of the most important factors to consider in helping others achieve heightened consciousness. When acting as a guide, speak slowly, clearly, and soothingly.

Let your words come out at a measured, even pace, almost as if you were following a metronome's beat; avoid rushed phrases, or pauses that give the impression that you are searching for the right word.

Students will usually have their eyes closed while you are speaking, so they cannot watch your lips or your gestures. All that reaches them is the sound of your voice, and they should not have to strain to hear it.

Try to maintain a calm, soothing tone that communicates trust, comfort, and relaxation.

Choice of Music

Select music that easily generates good, warm feelings in the listeners. For a first session I would suggest music such as "Venus" from Holst's *The Planets*, Aaron Copland's *Appalachian Spring* (the last third of the record which includes the recapitulation of the original theme), or Debussy's *Afternoon of a Faun*. Such easy and universally satisfying music will go far to ensure a successful listening experience. The secret of success in listening is to enter deeply into one's own emotional life; and for this purpose, music with slight rather than major mood shifts is most satisfying to the listener. The pieces recommended above have this unobtrusive but supportive quality.

At the beginning, choose music that is likely to be unfamiliar to students. Experimenters have found that the best way to help people get inside themselves and use their emotional faculties is to play music that is not well known to them. There are good reasons for using either familiar or non-familiar music, but for the sample induction presented here, which emphasizes affective imagery, non-familiar music is preferable.

Normally, students do not need to know either the name of the selection or its composer before the listening session. Such details constitute distractions, especially when the objective of the exercise is emotion-centered. After the exercise, however, students who had deep and satisfying experiences while listening may want references to the title and composer.

Students, especially younger ones, like to give descriptive names or titles to their listening experiences. A title gives them an easy way to recall the experience or refer to it in discussion.

Sample High School Classroom Induction: "Going to a Favorite Place."

Remembering to speak slowly, clearly and soothingly, this is how one might present this exercise in a junior high classroom:

Everybody has a favorite place
where they like to go.

Perhaps for you
it is a corner of your own room
that you have fixed up
just the way you like;
or perhaps there is a place outside,
maybe in a tree or near a bush,
or in a corner of your yard.
Or perhaps you have a special place that you go to
in your imagination
when you want to be
alone with your thoughts;
and perhaps in your mind
you've painted a picture of this place.
For some people.
it is a place they see in their dreams.

But wherever it is,
I would like to have you
think of a place like this—
a place you feel is yours,
where you feel that you can be yourself,
where you like to be.
Or maybe for you
it is not a specific place,
but some activity that you enjoy doing,
like hunting in the woods in the fall.
I would like you to capture the feeling
that goes with it—
the feeling of enjoyment
in your place, or in your activity.

Now, keeping this place in mind,
we are going to go through
some relaxation suggestions.
They will help you to
get to your favorite place more easily.

First, close your eyes.
Now, sitting in your chair,
put yourself in the most relaxed position you can.
You may want to put your head
down on your desk,
or just let it lean forward a little . . .
whatever makes you comfortable.
For many people the most relaxed position
is sitting up rather straight,
so that the bones and muscles
are in their normal positions.

Let your arms be relaxed,
your feet flat on the floor,
and the weight of your body
comfortably resting on the seat of your chair.
Perhaps you would like to move about a little
until you feel just right.
Then, with your eyes closed,
let a sense of peace and relaxation
come over you
until you feel relaxed all over.
As soon as you feel relaxed,
and I think that most of you are by now,
let your mind go out of the schoolroom
and directly to your special place.
It won't take long.
It will just take a moment.
And meanwhile we'll just wait.
I'll wait for you to get there.

Ah, there we are.

Familiarize yourself with everything around you.
Now that you are in this place
that you enjoy so much,
I'll deepen the experience for you

by counting from ten to zero.
As I count from ten to zero
you will go more and more deeply
into the experience;
you will feel the colors,
and you will feel other sensations
that you ordinarily associate with this experience.
And when I get to zero
and you are deeply into this experience,
then listen to the music
that I'll play for you.

The music will take you
more and more into the experience,
and you will be able
to experience more and more and
in greater depth.
The music may take you to many places
and that will be fine, too.
And then, when the music stops,
I will count from one to ten
and you will come back from your experience,
and you will be able to share it with one another.

All right. Now we will begin.
You are in your favorite place
and as I count you will go
deeper and deeper into the experience,
and let the music take you
Wherever you wish to go.
Ten, nine, deeper, deeper.
Eight, seven,
more and more deeply into the experience.
Six, feeling very relaxed, very happy.
Five, four, more and more,
deeper and deeper.

Three, two, feeling very good.
One, very deeply into the experience.
Zero.
And now listen to the music,
and let it take you
wherever it wants to take you.

At this point begin a music selection lasting from seven to ten minutes, with a simple emotion-producing content. Wait quietly while the record plays, observing the reactions of the students. When the selection has concluded, remove the phonograph arm from the record, and say—in a quiet, soothing voice:

The music has ended
and you have all had interesting experiences
that I know you will want to share.
Now I will count from one to ten,
and when I reach ten
you'll feel alert,
back in the classroom
and eager to share your experiences.

One, two, remembering your experiences,
eager to share them.
Three, four, becoming more and more alert.
Five, six, alert, back to normal.
Seven, feeling very good about your experiences.
Eight, nine, ten, wide awake,
eager to share with one another.

Sharing the Experience

Most students will have a satisfying and novel listening experience. A few will go into very deep states of altered consciousness; others will not enter it at all. Don't let this disturb you. They may be frightened and "know" that they are not yet ready for it. Or they may have deliberately chosen not to let the music affect them—perhaps to see how altered consciousness affects others, or perhaps just to be stubborn.

Once such students see their friends sharing experiences after the exercise, chances are they will be more cooperative on the next occasion.

Be sure to allow sufficient time for group-sharing; don't play a selection that ends just a minute or two before the bell rings.

Encourage the young people to express themselves. Let them feel free to describe their experiences, however bizarre or mundane they may be. If you can get several of the more outgoing ones to describe their experiences first, the others will probably feel freer to say: "Something similar happened to me."

As students become more adept at the new experience, extend the listening time by adding a second or third selection. You may also try longer pieces involving increasingly dynamic emotional changes, until the class is ready to deal with music that expresses a variety of moods.

Exercise: Programmatic Music

In addition to the general suggestions, it is possible to build listening experiences around programmatic music stories. *Peter and The Wolf, Petrouska,* and *The Nutcracker Suite* are obvious examples.

When listening in states of altered consciousness, the imagination becomes very active and creative. Hence, rather than telling the entire story of, for example, *The Nutcracker,* I suggest you simply tell the students enough to meet the characters and visualize the setting. Then let the music unfold a story in the consciousness of each student.

The elements of the story can be found on the album jacket. For example, from the *Nutcracker* jacket, written by Herbert Glass, you might read this paragraph to the class:

It is the night before Christmas; snow is gently falling. We enter a comfortable mid-19th-century German home. The councillor, his wife, and close relations are putting the finishing touches to a brightly-lit Christmas tree and various other seasonal decorations. The couple's children, Clara and Fritz, and their many little friends play on the floor, trying to guess at the contents of the Christmas packages under the trees. With charming gravity, the orchestra strikes up a march and the children come forward to receive their presents.

These lines provide enough of a setting for the students to generate their own fantasies.

After the music, encourage them to tell their versions of the story as they heard the music tell it. After a number of them have described their versions, you may want to read them the original story which Tchaikovsky set to music.

It is important to encourage students to develop their *own* story and not to have them feel that they must guess what the *real* story is. The latter approach could generate feelings of inadequacy in the child, whereas the fact that he created a totally different story assures him of his creativity.

Here are some programmatic selections, including operas, for children:

Dukas: The Sorcerer's Apprentice
      : Peer Gynt Suite

Prokofiev: Peter and the Wolf
Rimski-Korsakov: Scheherezade
Stravinski: Petrouchka
Strauss, Richard: Til Eulenspiegel's Merry Pranks
Tchaikovsky: Swan Lake
Bizet: Carmen
Humperdinck: Hansel and Gretel
Menotti: Amahl and the Night Visitors
Verdi: Aida

Exercise: Scenic Titles

The five parts of Grofe's *Grand Canyon Suite* are:

1. *Sunrise*
2. *Painted Desert*
3. *On the Trail*
4. *Sunset*
5. *Cloudburst*

For students who have already experienced the new way to music and are ready to listen to the *Grand Canyon Suite*, a few words about each title are enough to generate a satisfying disposition for listening.

Exercise: Space Trips

Holst's *Planets* has proved an especially successful vehicle for those in altered states of consciousness. As with Grofe's *Grand Canyon Suite*, most of the Holst's titles, alone, are almost enough to provide a satisfying setting for listening:

Venus, The Bringer of Peace
Mercury, The Winged Messenger
Jupiter, The Bringer of Jollity
Uranus, The Magician
Neptune, The Mystic

Avoid Mars, The Bringer of War, which tends to provoke hostility and anxiety; also Saturn, The Bringer of Old Age, which might be unattractive to children.

Appendix A

Towards a theory of Consciousness and Music

Conceptual Model of States of Consciousness

Most psychologists have a schema of the human mind to help describe experiences in nonordinary states of consciousness.

The conceptual framework that underlies the thinking in this new way to music, roughly based on the psychosynthesis model of Roberto Assagioli, involves four levels of mind. (See Figure 1.) Following Assagioli, the bottom layer is called the *lower unconscious*. It contains the elementary physiological or psychosomatic activities which direct the coordination of bodily functions, the fundamental drives, and the roots of various pathological states such as phobias, obsessions, compulsions, and delusions. The material which a psychotherapist seeks to uncover with a patient often involves areas of the lower unconscious. Therapy supported by music has been found very helpful in probing many hard-to-reach areas on this level.

The next level is simply labeled the *unconscious* (the Middle Unconscious in Assagioli's schema). It holds the impulses, habits, and conflicts of which we are unaware, and which are a source of many of the problems of ordinary life.

This level also contains psychological material similar to that of our waking consciousness and relatively easily accessible to it, such as the motor reflexes of driving a car, or the manual movements involved in tying a shoelace.

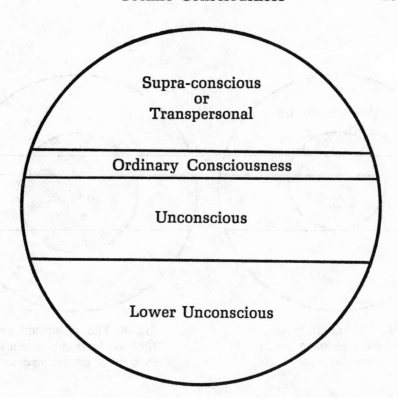

Fig. 1. Levels of Consciousness.

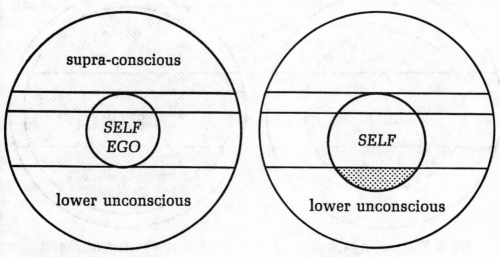

Fig. 2. The circle of self, or ego, in the ordinary field of consciousness.

Fig. 3. The circle of self reaching into the lower unconscious through psychotherapy.

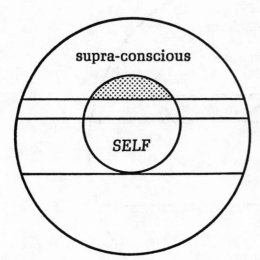

Fig. 4. The creative self, or genius, free to move in the supraconscious.

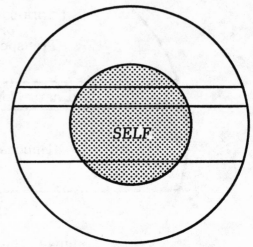

Fig. 5. The observing self that is learning to move in a new consciousness.

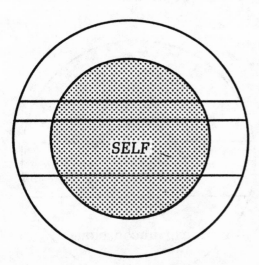

Fig. 6. The self in expanding consciousness, free to move in all levels.

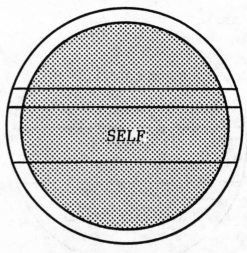

Fig. 7. The self in almost complete consciousness.

The next mental layer is that of *ordinary consciousness*, and the diagram emphasizes how little of our mental activity actually belongs to that level.

The top level, the area that is of primary concern in *Music and Your Mind*, may be called the *supraconscious* or the *transpersonal* (the Higher Unconscious or Superconscious according to the theory of psychosynthesis theory). This region of the mind contains material from which we derive creative insight and higher order drives. In Roberto Assagioli's words:

From this region we receive our higher intuitions and inspirations—artistic, philosophical or scientific, ethical "imperatives" and urges to humanitarian and heroic action. It is the source of the higher feelings, such as altruistic love; of genius and of the states of contemplation, illumination, and ecstasy. In this realm are latent the higher psychic functions and spiritual energies.

The boundary of supra-consciousness (the large circle in the diagram) should not be conceived as fixed and firm, but rather like a porous membrane that can stretch into vaster regions, which may be called *cosmic consciousness*. Included in this outer region would be what Jung called the collective unconscious and archetypal material.

The Conscious Self

The smaller, inner circle (see Figure 2) refers to the *self* or *ego*—that part of the personality with which we are in touch. It includes the images, feelings, ideas, desires, which we can directly experience, observe, analyze, and judge.

For many people, the circle of self involves material from only the unconscious and ordinary consciousness (Fig. 2). For them, any experience outside of the ordinary waking state may be called a new consciousness or, technically, an *altered state of consciousness.* The self of the creative person often reaches up into the supra-conscious, to various degrees of insight, higher motivation, and religious experience (Fig. 4).

With new techniques, persons can learn to expand their awareness of self into both the upper and lower levels of consciousness, so that the self learns to move freely from one dimension to the other (Fig. 5). Many LSD experiences are examples of reaching new levels of consciousness. Psychedelic drugs, however, are only one of many techniques for reaching altered states of consciousness.

Hopefully, with the development of newer techniques for reaching other levels of the mind, the self can slowly expand (Fig. 6) and, by a kind of psychological osmosis, begin to realize ever more completely the mind's fullest potential (Fig. 7).

This process of expanding self-awareness develops in successive stages. First, the person locates and identifies his own smaller circle. He experiences his own presence there, he becomes conscious of his own self-awareness.

Next, this ego or self learns to observe the rest of the functioning in the inner circle. The *observing self* slowly learns to operate with greater maturity.

Once the ego has begun to use the capacities in the smaller circle, the person can begin to expand his observing capacities into the lower level of the large circle. There, in the unconscious part of the mind, observing and dealing with its symbols and images, the self can begin to work on unresolved personal conflict.

When the observing self is operating outside ordinary consciousness, it may also enter the supra-conscious area. Here the images and symbols are different from those encountered in the lower unconscious. There they expressed conflict and struggle; here they are open, vast, unencumbered, intuitive. There the self worked to change feelings and images, here the images seem to be unalterable, the feelings untouchable. The material in the lower unconscious seems very personal, the supra-conscious content is often spoken of as transpersonal. It is characterized by a certain timelessness and universality, which excludes personal issues and problems.

Music without Drugs

Experience and research at the Maryland Psychiatric Research Center had demonstrated that drugs and music together formed a powerful team, enabling the observing self to reach new levels of awareness. Music seemed to intensify the drug's effect. But, it may also be that the drug is intensifying the music's effect. It was known that the individual effects of LSD and of music, though similar in some respects, could be isolated: A theory was needed to explain why the two were so effective together.

Therapists saw LSD as principally, though not exclusively, opening (and keeping open for a number of hours) the doors to expanded consciousness, and music as principally, though not exclusively, providing the guiding structure for the personal inner exploration.

For some, interest lay in demonstrating that patients could reach extraordinary states and work
through their problems with the help of music alone.
The problem lay in finding a means of helping the
observing self pass through the defenses and busy-
ness of ordinary consciousness into a new consciousness, so that the person could be intensely involved
in a music experience at deeper levels of his being.
The hypothesis was that, should such a means be
developed, experiences similar to those induced by
the drug would be attained. Furthermore, non-drug
approaches to the unconscious would be more acceptable in general, not only because of the current
national drug-scene scare, but because they would be
less demanding on both the patient and the therapist.

A method of altering consciousness developed by
Hanscarl Leuner, called Guided Affective Imagery
(GAI) lends itself to preparing a patient for evocation
of visual imagery and has been found to be thera-
peutically effective. Leuner describes his technique
thus:

The patient lies down on a couch. Outer stimuli
are reduced as much as possible. The room should
be quiet and the lights dimmed. He is then asked
to relax. It may be advisable to offer some verbal
suggestions that help to deepen the relaxation. The
therapist then starts with the first standard situa-
tion, the meadow. The patient is asked to imagine
a meadow, any meadow that comes to mind. No
further comment is given. Everything is left as open
and as unstructured as possible so that the patient
can develop his own image of a meadow with its
associated feeling quality. The therapist gently
persists in asking the patient to give detailed de-

scriptions of his imagery and of the feelings associated with it. The therapist is, so to speak, always the companion of the patient in his world of imagery.

Originally, GAI was used without music, but recently appropriate music has been added by Leuner, by Cecil Chamberlin and William Trussell at the Menninger Clinic in Topeka, and by William Richards and John Lobell at the Maryland Center. All report that music enhances the efficacy of the GAI technique.

Therapists found, then, that music listened to in an altered state of consciousness is helpful for psychiatric patients. This gave rise to the insight—though it only occurred much later—that if music is good for patients, it might be as good or even better for mentally healthy people—an insight which ultimately led to this book.

Appendix B

The Mood Wheel

The specific mood or emotional expression communicated by a particular musical composition is of considerable importance in planning a program of music for listening in altered states of consciousness.

Selections with well-integrated and clearly focused moods seem to have a greater effect upon people in altered states than music with frequent or abrupt mood changes.

The mood wheel, an arrangement of 66 adjectives in eight related groups, was developed by Kate Hevner for classifying emotional expressions of musical selections.

The eight groups of adjectives are arranged around an imaginary circle in such a way that (1) the adjectives in one group are closely related to and compatible with each other; (2) any two adjacent groups have some characteristics in common; and (3) groups at diagonally opposite points of the circle are as unlike each other as possible. Mood transitions between adjacent groups are made without abrupt or awkward changes. The complete circle involves a wide range of the most common affective experiences.

To test individual musical pieces for the moods they communicate, a group of subjects listen to the selection, then check the mood adjective group that they feel most corresponds to the mood of the musical selection.

Some selections strike a common response in most listeners; such selections will have predictably clear

ARRANGEMENT OF ADJECTIVES FOR RECORDING THE MOOD EFFECT OF MUSIC*

6
merry
joyous
gay
happy
cheerful
bright

7
exhilarated
soaring
triumphant
dramatic
passionate
sensational
agitated
exciting
impetuous
restless

5
humorous
playful
whimsical
fanciful
quaint
sprightly
delicate
light
graceful

4
lyrical
leisurely
satisfying
serene
tranquil
quiet
soothing

8
vigorous
robust
emphatic
martial
ponderous
majestic
exalting

1
spiritual
lofty
awe-inspiring
dignified
sacred
solemn
sober
serious

2
pathetic
doleful
sad
mournful
tragic
melancholy
frustrated
depressing
gloomy
heavy
dark

3
dreamy
yielding
tender
sentimental
longing
yearning
pleading
plaintive

*Kate Hevner, "An Experimental Study of the Affective Value of Sounds and Poetry." *American Journal of Psychology*, 1937, **49**, 419–434.

Table 1
THE RELATIONSHIP BETWEEN INDIVIDUAL SELECTIONS AND PREDOMINANT MOODS

Selections	Chi-square	Mood Wheel Group(s)	Predominant Moods
1. Til Eulenspiegel, Strauss	4.58	8,5	Vigorous, Playful
2. Introduction and Allegro, Ravel	17.951*	3	Tender
3. "I Believe," Mahalia Jackson	20.938**	1	Solemn
4. A Love Supreme, John Coltrane	19.336**	6	Gay
5. "El Condor," Simon and Garfunkel	6.7164	6,5	Gay, Playful
6. Rite of Spring, Stravinsky	14.628	7	Exciting
7. "Deep River," Norman Luboff Choir	11.78	1,2	Solemn, Sad
8. Mouldau, Smetana	6.36	4	Leisurely
9. "The Psychologically Ultimate Seashore"	6.52	—	None
10. Pines of Rome, "Gianicola," Respighi	16.88*	4	Leisurely
11. Misa Criolla (Folk Mass)	28.00***	6	Gay

12. Fanfare from "La Peri," Dukas	28.435***	8	Vigorous
13. "Swan of Tuonela," Sibelius	16.389*	2	Sad
14. "Good Shepherd," Volunteers	12.254	6	Gay
15. Firebird Suite, "Finale," Stravinsky	14.193	7	Exciting
16. Der Rosenkavalier, Act 3, Duet, J. Strauss	11.918	4,3,2	Leisurely, Tender, Sad
17. Appalachian Spring, Copland	12.6505	4	Leisurely
18. "Evening Prayer," Humperdinck	42.953***	1	Solemn
19. Missa Luba, "Sanctus"	8.437	1	Solemn
20. Jesus Christ Super Star, "Chorus," Webber and Rice	14.074	6	Gay
21. Organ swell	8.397	7	Exciting
22. Tapestry, "Sonata in G minor," Bach	7.834	5	Playful
23. Songs of the Auvergne, "Brezariola," Canteloube	10.158	2	Sad

Level of Statistical significance
*** $p = <.001$ (d.f. $= 8$): 26.12 or higher.
** $p = <.01$ (d.f. $= 8$): 20.09 or higher.
* $p = <.05$ (d.f. $= 8$): 15.51 or higher.

mood-communication when listened to in altered consciousness. A selection that evokes in listeners a range of responses indicates a piece whose mood tends to be diffuse or nonspecific. Pieces having this nonspecific quality may be of value at certain stages of heightened-consciousness listening.

Three different groups (Total N = 65) composed of college and ghetto high school students were asked to classify according to the mood wheel short portions of twenty-three selections of music. While listening, they were asked to select the one adjective-group on the wheel that seemed to them most descriptive of the musical selection they had just heard. Few, if any, in the total population would be considered sophisticated music listeners.

The results of the study indicate that in the subjects' minds there exists a strong relationship between a musical selection and the mood associated with it.

Statistically, the Contingency Coefficient was used to test the general relationship between mood and music over all the selections and all the subjects. The resulting Contingency Coefficient (CC = .75) was found to be highly significant at the .001 level (d.f. = 66).

A further analysis of the relationship between mood and music was made on the twenty-three individual selections using the Cochran Q Test. As can be seen from Table I, the mood associations for four selections (3, 11, 12, 18) are strikingly high; here the Chi-Squares, which range from 20.9 to 42.09, are significant beyond the .01 level (d.f. = 8). Four additional selections (2, 4, 10, 13) are significant beyond the .05 level. Closely approaching significance were selections 6, 15, 20.

Some sample arrays of responses are presented in the following histograms. Selection 1, Til Eulenspiegel by Strauss, demonstrates two clear mood peaks, at Vigorous and Playful. Selection 2, Introduction and Allegro by Ravel, illustrates a close clustering of sad and leisurely about a central mood, Tender. Selection 3 indicates a very precise mood association, where almost all responses fall into a single category, Solemn.

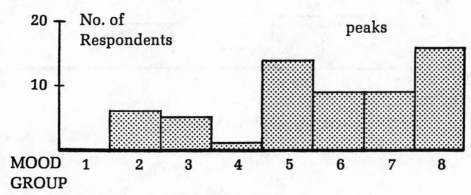

Selection 1. by Strauss

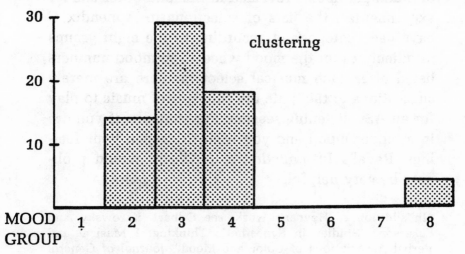

Selection 2. by Ravel

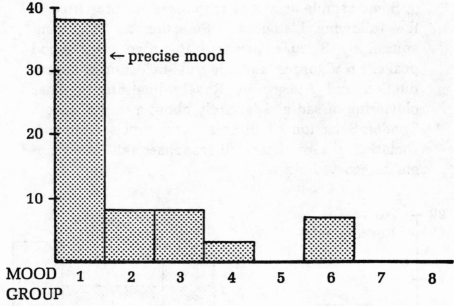

40

30 ← precise mood

20

10

MOOD 1   2   3   4   5   6   7   8
GROUP

Selection 3. by Mahalia Jackson

Because of the significant associative tendencies of mood and music revealed in this and other similar experiments*, the lists of selections in Appendix C have been categorized according to the eight groups of adjectives on the mood wheel. The mood numbers listed after each musical selection there are merely suggestions to facilitate the choosing of music to play for an ASC listening session. For example, if you are in a tender mood and you wish to deepen your feelings, Ravel's *Introduction and Allegro* would probably be very helpful.

*In addition to Hevner's work, see Odbert, Karowsky, and Eckerson, "Studies in Synesthetic Thinking: I Musical and Verbal Associations of Color and Mood," *Journal of General Psychology*, 1942, *26*, 153–173.

Appendix C

Suggested Recordings for Altered States of Consciousness Experience

The appropriate choice of music is of greatest importance in opening the doors of perception to self-understanding and inner experience. It has been discovered that some of the music selections listed in the first edition of *Music and Your Mind* have remained effective for use in Guided Imagery and Music experience and other selections have not. This awareness has led to the present revision. This appendix includes music exclusively from the classical repertoire, which we have found most deeply accesses imagery of a healing nature. To facilitate successful music choices, the listing below is given alphabetically by composer, followed by title of composition, time-length of each selection, mood designation, and a short comment.

The numbers in the mood column correspond to the eight mood clusters discussed in the previous appendix and refer to the predominant mood-communications of the selection.

Summarily:

1 – spiritual
2 – sad
3 – dreamy
4 – lyrical
5 – playful
6 – joyous
7 – exciting
8 – vigorous

From these listings single selections may be chosen or a variety of programs may be developed for specific group or individual needs. As a courtesy, The Bonny Foundation offers for professional use a series of prerecorded tape programs: for generating positive affect, peak experience, imagery, quiet music, comforting/ analytic, group experience, nurturing and other effective themes. These tapes include many, but not all of the selections listed in Appendix C. To locate various recordings of these works, consult the Schwann Catalog in your library or record store.

Composer and Title	Time	Mood*	Comments
Albinoni, *Adagio in G minor*	6:52	1,2	Organ and strings create color diversity
Bach, *Arioso*	5:00	4	transpersonal
Bach, *Air for the G String* from *Suite #3*	5:45	1,3	Warm string melodic tonality
Bach, *Jesu, Joy of Man's Desiring*	3:41	3	Stokowski instrumental transcriptions add a
Sheep May Safely Graze	5:37	4	patina to Bach through orchestral color and
Little Fugue in G	3:50	6	tone
Come Sweet Death	5:50	2,3	" "
Sarabande, Violin Partita in B minor	4:30	3,4	" "
Christmas Oratorio, Shepherd's Song	9:29	1	" "
Bach, *Toccata and Fugue in D minor*	9:32	7,8	" "
Bach, *Toccata, Adagio & Fugue in C major*	5:12	8,1	building to peak
Bach, *Concerto for Two Violins*	7:38		
Allegro		5,6	energy, assurance, security, canon-style
Largo ma non tanto		3,4	interweaving of solo voices
Bach, *Sarabande from English Suite #3*	5:23	1-3	guitar warmth, sincerity
Bach-Stokowski, *Preludium in E major*	3:45	6,7	exciting, dramatic

* see Appendix B

Composer and Title	Time	Mood	Comments
Barber, *Adagio for Strings*	6:21	1,7	broad sonority, build-up to deeply moving climax
Beethoven, *Piano Concerto #5* Adagio, un poco mosso, B major	6:36	4,5	delicate, fragile, takes us to another world.
Beethoven, *Piano Concerto #3* Largo	13:00	4	comfort and hope
Beethoven, Scene by the Brook Andante molto moto, from *Symphony #6*	11:53	4	evokes images of country scenes
Beethoven, *Romance for Violin and Orchestra in F major*	8:00	4,7	tender passion
Beethoven, *Violin Concerto in D minor* Larghetto	8:38	3,7	timeless flow of consciousness
Beethoven, Arietta, adagio molto semplice cantabile, from *Sonata #32 in C minor*	17:23	3,7	salutary to the body
Beethoven, *Symphony #9* Adagio molto e cantabile	14:47	1,4	to experience life transitions
Berlioz, *Harold in Italy* Procession of Pilgrims	7:28	4	viola color, travel, movement

	Time		Description
Berlioz, *Symphony Fantastique*			
A Ball	8:00	6,7	waltz, romance dialogue between oboe,
Scene in the Country	18:00	4,7	English horn, tranquility
Berlioz, *L'enfance du Christ*			
Flight into Egypt	11:00	4	suggests travel, vocal chorus
The Shepherd's Farewell to the Holy Family	4:00	3	
Boccherini, *Cello Concerto in B flat major* Adagio, non troppo	6:57	3,2	graceful, yearning
Brahms, *Symphony #1*			
Un poco Allegretto e grazioso	4:25	5,6	graceful movement
Brahms, *Symphony #3*			
Poco Allegretto	5:29	2	tender, dreamy, sad, nostalgic
Brahms, *Symphony #4*			
Andante moderato	12:40	4,7	appropriate for a mini session
Brahms, *Double Concerto for Violin & Cello in A minor*	8:45	3	dialogue between string voices
Brahms, *Violin Concerto in D minor*, Adagio	8:38	3,4	pure, intense, romantic
Brahms, *Piano Concerto #2*			
Andante-piu adagio	14:29	4,7	*unique, restful blending of cello piano & orchestra timbres.*
Brahms, The German Requiem			
Part I Poco Andante	5:00	1,2,8	choral, sonorous, reassurance.
Part V Andante	11:49		solo with choir, death & transcendence

Composer and Title	Time	Mood	Comments
Britten, *Simple Symphony* Sarabande	7:10	4,7	nurturing, yearning
Copland, *Appalachian Spring*	20:00	2-6	evokes imagery
Debussy, *Dances Sacred and Profane*	10:30	3,4,5	beginning imagery exercise
Debussy, *The Girl with the Flaxen Hair* *Sunken Cathedral*	2:50 4:00	3 2,7	youthful reminiscence evokes imagery
Debussy, Sirenes from *Nocturnes*	11:00	2,3,4	intense, mysterious voices used as instruments
Debussy, *Prelude to the Afternoon of a Fawn*	11:15	3,4	delicate, erotic beauty of dream world, relaxing
Debussy, *Clair de Lune*	5:15	4	depicts mystery & beauty of the moon
Delius, *In a Summer Garden*	14:55	4,5,6	prose melody against chromatic harmony, fanciful
Delius, Intermezzo & Serenade from *Hassan*	3:55	3,4	nostalgic, active sensuousness in music
Delius, *The Walk to the Paradise Garden*	8:40	3	nostalgic, active sensuousness in music

Piece	Time		Description
Delius, Intermezzo from *Fennimore and Gerda*	5:26	4	nostalgic, active sensuousness in music
Delius, *On Hearing the First Cuckoo in Spring*	5:44	3,4	nostalgic, active sensuousness in music
Delius, La Calinda from *Koanga*	4:03	5,6	nostalgic, active sensuousness in music
Dvorak, *Nocturne for Strings in B major*	7:32	3,4	yearning, resolution
Dvorak, Largo from *New World Symphony* 2nd movement	12:15	3,4	opening the heart center
Dvorak, Larghetto from *Four Romantic Pieces*	5:26	2,3	romance
Dvorak, Romanza from *Czech Suite*	5:12	3,4	serene, tender, satisfying
Elgar, *Enigma Variations*			
#8 W.N.	2:00	5	delicate, graceful, majestic, exalting, building to peak.
#9 Nimrod	3:00	1,8	
Faure, Paradisium from *Requiem*	2:56	1	sacred choral
Glinka, Aria from *Ivan Susanin*, Act IV	5:20	8,1	dramatic, intense, commanding, dark vocal color
Gounod, Offertory, Sanctus from *St. Cecilia Mass*	7:53	1,8	sacred vocal, can evoke peak experience
Haydn, Adagio from *Cello Concerto in C*	9:45	3,4	mothering, personal, caring

Composer and Title	Time	Mood	Comments
Holst, *The Planets*			entire suite evokes imagery, every mood category is included.
Mars, bringer of war	6:36	7,8	
Venus, bringer of peace	7:48	3,4	
Mercury, winged messenger	4:02	5,6	
Jupiter, bringer of jollity	7:55	6,7	
Saturn, bringer of old age	8:39	2,1	
Uranus, the magician	5:35	5,7	
Neptune, the mystic	8:07	1,4	
Mahler, Ruhevoll ("World Without Gravity") from *Symphony #4* exploration	23:25	4,7,8	quiet, inner
Mozart, *Vesperae Solemnes de Confessore, Laudate Dominum*	4:00	4,1	serene, sacred, vocal solo with orchestra & choir
Mussorgski-Ravel, Great Gate at Kiev, from *Pictures at an Exhibition*	5:00	7,8	exciting, dramatic
Pachelbel, *Canon in D*	7:09	4	ostinato creates secure ground for ASC
Pierne, *Concertstuck for Harp*	14:15	4,5,7	explores relationships
Rachmaninoff, Adagio from *Symphony #2*	10:00	3,4,5	romantic, tender, satisfying
Rachmaninoff, Adagio Sustenuto from *Piano Concerto #2*	9:53	3,4	romantic, sentimental

Piece	Time	Tracks	Notes
Ravel, *Daphnis and Chloe*, Suite #2 Beginning	7:21	8,4	evokes imagery
Ravel, *Introduction & Allegro*	11:00	4,5	harp & strings engage the listener
Ravel, *Pavan pour une infante defunte*	6:30	1,3	otherworldly, uplifting
Respighi, The Dove from *The Birds*	4:35	3,5	vibrant, delicate
Respighi, Gianicola, from *The Pines of Rome*	6:15	4	evokes imagery of nature
Schubert, Der Neugierige from *Die Schone Mullerin*	4:15	3	first love
Sibelius, *The Swan of Tuonela*	7:44	2,3	plaintive English horn moves and expands consciousness
Sibelius, Allegretto from *Symphony #2 in D*	11:28	5,7, 2,8	creative exploration
Smetana, *Die Moldau*	6:21	4,5,7	vigorous, physical, reminiscent of water travel
Strauss, *The Beautiful Blue Danube*	9:12	6	ultimate joyous movement
Strauss, Transfiguration from *Death and Transfiguration*	4:00	1	transfiguration
Tchaikovsky, Waltz of Flowers from *The Nutcracker Suite*	20:00	4,5,6	fanciful, graceful movement
Tchaikovsky, Canzonetta from *Violin Concerto*	5:00	3,4,7	longing, passion

Composer and Title	Time	Mood	Comments
Tchaikovsky, Scherzo from *Symphony #4*	5:17	5	movement imagery
Tschesnekoff, *Salvation is Created*	6:00	1	profound, mystical
Vaughan Williams, *Fantasia on Greensleeves*	4:08	4,5	nostalgic, pastoral
Vaughan Williams, *Fantasia on a theme by Thomas Tallis*	16:15	3,4, 7,8	inner exploration
Vaughan Williams, Romanza from *Symphony #5*	12:37	4,7	evokes imagery
Vaughan Williams, *The Lark Ascending*	15:52	3,4	soaring violin, triumphant, tranquil
Vaughan Williams, *Rhosymedre*	3:55	3	tender, serene
Villa-Lobos, *Bachianas Brasilieras, #5*	5:53	4	lyrical voice as instrument
Vivaldi, *Concerto Grosso in D minor #11 Opus 3*	11:22	7,3,5	joy, abandonment
Vivaldi, Largo from *Concerto for Guitar and Orchestra in D*	4:13	3	thoughtful, tender
Vivaldi, Et in terra pax from *Gloria*	5:46	1	build to peak, long vocal crescendo
Wagner, Prelude to Act I from *Lohengrin*	9:50	1,4	gentle, build to peak
Wieniawski, Romance, Adagio-non troppo from	5:08	3,7	passionate

Suggested Further Reading:

Bonny, Helen L., *GIM Monograph 1: Facilitating GIM Sessions*. ICM Books, Baltimore, MD. 1978

Bonny, Helen L., *GIM Monograph 2: The Role of Taped Music Programs in the GIM process*. ICM Books, Baltimore, MD. 1978

Summer, Lisa, *GIM in the Institutional Setting*. MMB Press, St. Louis, MO., 1988

Other titles by Station Hill Press

PERCEPTION

The Reality Illusion: How You Make the World You Experience, Ralph Strauch, $10.95 paper.

TOUCH THERAPY

Where Healing Waters Meet: Touching Mind and Emotion Through the Body, Dr. Clyde Ford, Foreword by Marilyn Ferguson, $19.95 cloth.

Job's Body: A Handbook for Bodywork, Deane Juhan, Foreword by Ken Dychtwald, $29.95 cloth.

TRANSPERSONAL PSYCHOLOGY/ENERGETICS

Emotional First Aid: A Crisis Handbook, Sean Haldane, $9.95 paper.

Music and Sound in the Healing Arts: An Energy Approach, John Beaulieu, $11.95 paper, $19.95 cloth.

The Lover Within: Opening to Energy in Sexual Practice, Julie Henderson, $14.95 paper.

The Shaman's Doorway: Opening Imagination to Power and Myth, Stephen Larsen, $10.95 paper.

Dragon Rises, Red Bird Flies: Psychology and Chinese Medicine, Leon Hammer, M.D., Foreword by Ted Kaptchuk, $24.95 cloth.

MEDITATION

Self-Liberation Through Seeing With Naked Awareness: An Introduction to the Nature of One's Own Mind in the Tibetan Dzogchen Tradition, Translated with Commentary by John Reynolds, Foreword by Namkhai Norbu, $14.95 paper, $29.95 cloth.

The Cycle of Day and Night: An Essential Tibetan Text on the Practice of Contemplation, Namkhai Norbu, translated and edited by John Reynolds, $10.95 paper.

SELF-HEALING

Lupus Novice: Towards Self-Healing, Laura Chester, $10.95 paper, $16.95 cloth.

Abused: A Guide to Recovery for Adult Survivors of Mental/Physical Child Abuse, Dee Anna Parrish, $8.95 paper.

CHILDREN'S EDUCATION

Childmade: Awakening Children to Creative Writing, Cynde Gregory, $10.95 paper, $19.95 cloth.

Available in local bookstores or order direct from:

Station Hill Press
Barrytown, New York 12507

Music and Sound in the Healing Arts

An Energy Approach

John Beaulieu

How music affects life energy and healing.

An invaluable resource for teachers, students, and practicioners in all the healing arts.
ELISABETH MACRAE, M.D.

Great! Finally a book on the important topic of healing with sound that comes from clinical experience--not facile esoteric speculation.... His experience as a therapist, composer and seeker come together to make this book a relevant, readable, and, most importantly, PRACTICAL introductory guide for the use of sound and music in healing.
DAVID GONZALEZ
Certified Music Therapist,
New York University

Artfully done and maintained by a well supported and cohesive systems view.
JAMES Z. SAID, D.C., N.D.,
President,
American Polarity Therapy Association

It is both a healing and an excitement to read this book!
STEFFIE YOST, D.C.

Almost everybody knows the power of music and environmental sound to affect our mood, emotions, memories, and sense of well-being. Here at last is a book that shows us in depth how to make use of our life-long experience of sound and turn it into a healing art. The result of such conscious use of sound and music is enhanced life-energy and wellness. The heart of the matter is energy and how its patterns (music is patterned energy) affect the body/ mind. Richly illustrated with pictures, stories, and the author's experiences as composer and therapist, the book explores the history and practice of healing sound from ancient philosophies to the practical applications of therapy, religion

and art: mantra, toning, voice evaluation, tuning forks, and music listening. It also contains guidelines and exercises for teaching and an evaluation of music therapy today.

John Beaulieu, active as composer, pianist, music therapist, and naturopathic doctor, is the founder and director of the Polarity Wellness Center and the Sound School of New York. A graduate in music of Indiana University, he has studied extensively in Eastern and Western healing systems, including acupuncture, polarity, and cranial therapy, ayruvedic medicine, nutrition, and psychotherapy. Formerly Supervisor of Activity Therapy at Bellevue Psychiatric and Assistant Professor at City University of New York.

$19.95 cloth, 0-88268-057-9,
$11.95 paper, 0-88268-056-0,
160 pages, 6 1/2 x 9 1/4,
illustrated, photos, charts, notes, bibliography,
HEALTH, MUSIC, THERAPY

The Shaman's Doorway

Opening Imagination to Power and Myth

Stephen Larsen
Foreword by Joan Halifax

Mythology, philosophy, psychology, and religion are all brought to illuminate how the Shaman's vision can open our own awareness in this expanded edition of the 1976 classic.

An excellent analytical and harmonizing survey.... He writes well, with a certain personal quality that gives life to the work throughout.... Mr. Larsen has opened (for me, at least) a lot of windows to the most recent of my contemporaries.

JOSEPH CAMPBELL

The Shaman's Doorway ranks with the more popular work of Mircea Eliade and Joseph Campbell, and their voices, together with C. G. Jung's, reverberate throughout. A fine book -- informed, intelligent, suggestive.

KIRKUS REVIEWS

Shamanism represents a body of knowledge that is pertinent to the ailments of contemporary society. Dr. Larsen guides us through this legacy with skill and ease, teaching us how the shaman's vision can expand our own awareness.

DR. STANLEY KRIPPNER

This book is of first-class quality, and should be read by all students of mythology, religion, philosophy, and psychology.

CHOICE

Widely celebrated, highly influential, and now expanded from the 1976 edition, this book was the first to interpret the ancient practice of the traditional Shaman from a distinctly modern, psychological perspective. The startling result lends a new understanding to the "inner journey" of our own time. Building on the works of Carl Jung and Joseph Campbell, Larsen offers

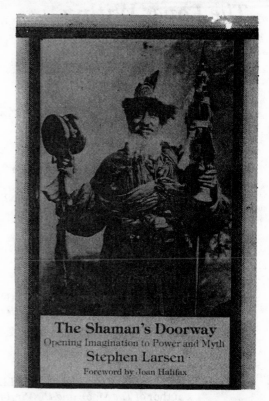

The Shaman's Doorway
Opening Imagination to Power and Myth
Stephen Larsen
Foreword by Joan Halifax

readers a methodology for traveling through "stages of mythic engagement"-- the encounter with spiritual power, death and rebirth, and the gaining of mystical vision--leading to the highest level of dialogue with the imagination: the way of the creative artist, the visionary warrior, and the modern shaman.

Stephen Larsen, a noted psychotherapist, teacher, author, and an editor of Chrysalis, *is co-originator of a shamanic technique of healing with masks. He lives in New Paltz, New York.*

$10.95 paper, ISBN 0-88268-072-2
260 pages, 6x9
25 photos of shamanistic materials, notes, bibliography, index
PSYCHOLOGY, SPIRITUAL PRACTICE

The Lover Within
Opening to Energy in Sexual Practice
Julie Henderson

Transforming intimacy with 63 exercises to be done alone or with a partner.

The Lover Within raises sexuality to another level. At last we have **Western Tantra**, and it's wonderful.

> **TSULTRIM ALLIONE**
> author of *Women of Wisdom*

Invaluable to anyone concerned with enriching their personal lives, including the sex therapists, psychotherapists and others who would help them do it.

> **PAUL EKMAN**
> author of *Telling Lies*

Finally, salvation from sex-as-it's-supposed-to-be.... Julie Henderson's book could—dare I say it—change the world from the inside out.

> **NOR HALL**
> author of *The Moon and the Virgin*

the lover within

OPENING TO ENERGY IN SEXUAL PRACTICE

julie henderson

The Lover Within opens us to the possibilities of energy in sexual and intimate life. It offers a straight-forward account of Julie Henderson's own approach to the enhancement and conscious use of energy aimed at creating sympathetic power between people. The focus is not on manipulative techniques but on the processes of energy itself: how to experience it, move it, collect it, heighten it, and share it toward deeper satisfaction and personal transformation. What was previously known only through secret and esoteric practice comes here into the public domain not as a part of an Eastern system requiring special mastery, but in a new and very Western language of direct experience rooted in the body. What comes out is a fresh approach to understanding what happens between lovers–and people in general. This book can alter both how we think about love and sex and what we do in intimate practice. The 63 practical exercises, to be done alone or with a partner, can bring us into contact with energetic processes and grant a measure of choice in regulating and altering it. Sexuality becomes the laboratory of transformation.

Julie Henderson, Ph.D., drawing on education and training in theater, therapy, counselling, psychology, somatics, Ericksonian hypnotherapy, and martial arts, offers training that emphasizes direct pleasure in being. She lives in Sydney, Australia, and gives workshops and consultations around the world.

$18.95 cloth, ISBN 0-88268-023-4,
$8.95 paper, ISBN 0-88268-049-8,
132 pages, 6x9,
line drawings, notes, bibliography,
PSYCHOLOGY , SEXUALITY

Dragon Rises, Red Bird Flies

Psychology and Chinese Medicine

Leon Hammer, M.D.

Foreword by Ted Kaptchuk

Psychology as the Western key to the oldest holistic medicine, healing through the energetic union of mind and body.

—is an excellent piece of work, and I would recommend it to anyone with a serious interest in Oriental medicine.

> **DR. PETER ECKMAN**
> Chairman, Schools Subcommittee of the California Acupuncture Examining Committee

Dr. Leon Hammer has written what might be termed a psychology primer for acupuncturists and other practitioners interested in Oriental medicine, its philosophy and its practices.... A treasure house of observations.

> **DR. MARK D. SEEM**
> author of *Bodymind Energetics: Toward a Dynamic Model of Health* and *Acupuncture Energetics*

In a revolutionary approach this American psychiatrist proposes understanding Chinese medicine through psychological eyes as "a congenial system of healing that embodies unification of body and mind, spirit and material, nature and man, philosophy and reality." Leon Hammer shows this Eastern practice – as much psychotherapy as physical medicine, as much a spiritual science as a physical one— to be a personal, subtle, yet highly technical medical system, allowing the physician to remain close to the life force in himself and others while providing an exacting diagnosis. Disease is seen not as an abstract and detached phenomenon, but as a maladaptive restitution, an attempt to heal that miscarries, a retreat from in-

tolerable or unsolvable problems, and an event aimed at staying intact and in contact. The book is a comprehensive, lucid presentation of detailed and direct experience, providing a new model for appreciating the traditional Chinese healer's effective and profound respect for individual integrity and energetic balance. It is easily accessible to the layman yet serves as a resource for the professional in any of the healing arts.

Leon Hammer, M.D., is a graduate of Cornell Medical College and the William A. White Institute of Psychoanalysis and Psychiatry, who studied Chinese medicine in England, China, and New York and has been practicing it for 17 years.

$24.95 cloth, ISBN 0-88268-062-5
400 pages, 6x9
charts, illustrations, index, bibliography
HEALTH, PSYCHOLOGY, ACUPUNCTURE